# How to Patent and
## Finance Your Invention

Robert Hodam

How to Patent and Finance Your Invention

Copyright © 1993 Robert Hodam

All rights reserved.

# Contents

# About the Author

Robert Hodam was the CEO of Emerging Technologies Institute, chairman/CEO of Robert Hodam Technologies, Inc., and the founder of five start-up companies, including three overseas. During the course of these businesses, he licensed technology to or from numerous US and Japanese companies, including Standard Oil, Culligan International, Hitachi, Nihon Koden, Escagenetics, JR3, Masumoto Surgical, Midwest Dental, and Nitta Industries KK.

He has also had technology consulting contracts with the World Bank, the Asian Development Bank, the United Nations, the US Congress, the US State Department, the US Department of Energy, and various foreign governments.

Mr. Hodam is a graduate of Stanford University, University of Southern California, and Oklahoma State University, with degrees in engineering and business. He also holds patents in the areas of pharmaceuticals and medical devices.

# Acknowledgments

I wish to thank the many people who offered encouragement and the reviewers and the editors of this book.

The attorneys who acted as legal editors include Fred Greguras, Esq., Fenwick & West (Palo Alto); Wilson-Sonsini (Palo Alto); and Mark White, Esq., White & Altman (Menlo Park).

The reviewers included Dr. Robert Smiley, Dean, University of California Davis School of Management; and Dr. Michael Witt, Harvard School of Business.

The initial text editor was Edward T. Engle Jr., who is not only a fine editor but a friend and successful entrepreneur. The editor for this updated edition is Joni Wilson.

Thanks also go to the many inventors I have known over the years for the opportunity to work together and learn from them. They have provided enjoyable and profitable experiences.

Finally, I wish to thank wife of forty-seven years Wendy and daughter Amy for their inspiration to commit my experiences in a written format.

# Preface

On humorist and social commentator Will Rogers's final resting place is written, "I never met a man I didn't like." Well, I can say I have never met an inventor I didn't like. But I haven't met many rich ones, either, which is a shame because we inventors are rarely appreciated and are always grossly underpaid. Unfortunately, the intellectual skills that make us inventive usually restrict our ability to convert our inventions into a profitable enterprise.

Inventors usually don't enjoy promoting ideas to investors or bankers, or otherwise raising money for manufacturing. Likewise, many inventors find selling their invention to a corporate buyer frustrating. It's just not their cup of tea. Consequently, they might end up with a patent but little in the bank—when they should be millionaires.

This book is intended for engineers and scientists, like me, who are inventors and wish to profit from their intellectual property. I have spent the last fifteen years buying patents, developing technologies from these patents, and selling the product or the developed technology, including developing and selling my own inventions.

Initially, my approach to making money from inventions was to create companies to manufacture products from the technology I had acquired. The first company I started was in the Philippines. I had acquired some proprietary trade secrets related to tropical forestry silviculture to increase lignin, cellulose, and other chemical production from a variety of tropical hardwoods.

I operated this company for six years under a government contract. Unfortunately for me, at the time I did not know how to protect my intellectual property. The silviculture methods we developed became the property of the government. This venture was a real lesson to me in the trade secret protection and maintaining a clear claim to ownership of intellectual property. I made money on the project itself but did not make anything from the inventions we developed because the US government ended up owning our technology.

My second venture was also in the Philippines. I acquired the rights to a technology to convert wood to a gas fuel (carbon monoxide-hydrogen) for use in engine generators. I tried to raise money to manufacture these units in the US, but no investor was willing to finance equipment for manufacturing. Investors insisted that in-house manufacturing tied up too much capital. They would only consider financing the company if I would contract out the manufacturing.

I got quotes from US machine shops, but they turned out to be too expensive. We couldn't afford to pay their price because the units would be too expensive for developing countries to buy. Consequently, I teamed up with a Philippine machine shop to manufacture the units, which we eventually sold throughout the South Pacific and Southeast Asia.

We knew patent infringements were difficult to prosecute in places like the Philippines. So, we decided to protect our intellectual property by making it difficult to "reverse engineer." Nevertheless, within two months after sales began, we learned of "copycat" units appearing on the market. These units, however, were not exactly like ours and did not incorporate the key features of our system that avoided engine fouling.

Consequently, the copycat units had terrible problems with engine fouling . . . so bad, in fact, that they gave our technology a bad name by association. We began to lose buyers because the copycats had produced such poor copies, so I licensed the technology rights to my Philippine manufacturer and cut my losses.

This experience was a real lesson in the risks a buyer of technology must face in developing an invention into a product and then taking it to market. I lost money on this acquisition because I could not control the competition or enforce intellectual property law regarding infringement.

This experience was also a lesson in reverse engineering. If your competition replicates your product well, you lose sales because they have a competitive product; and if they engineer your product poorly, your product might get a bad reputation by association. You lose sales either way. Always make sure you can protect your product.

At this point, I decided to abandon manufacturing and marketing in developing countries where I could not enforce intellectual property law. I decided to focus on acquiring technology for resale. In 1985, I opened an office in Tokyo with two Japanese partners. I bought and licensed technology in the US, then sold licenses to Japanese companies.

At this time, the Japanese had a huge appetite for foreign technology and were enforcing patents fairly well. We licensed medical devices, pharmaceuticals, robotics, biotechnology, and consumer appliances. Generally, I acquired my technology with a license to manufacture and market in Japan. I usually paid the inventor one dollar plus 10 percent of up-front and royalty payments I received from my sub-licensee. This business was successful and is the basis of most of my learning experience in foreign licensing and negotiating.

In 1989, it became clear to me that the Japanese speculative boom was about over and that a major recession was due in Japan. My partners also saw this coming, so we decided to pursue licensing and technology development in the US market.

Therefore, in 1990, I bought the marketing rights to a patented contact lens plastic from a US inventor and started a company to market this material and other polymer- based products for the medical industry. I also acquired an assignment (see Chapter Three) of another pharmaceutical polymer technology and began research on a third related product of my own.

The inventor of the contact lens technology was attempting to manufacture the plastic himself but was having many problems with quality control. Our sales were booming, but after numerous attempts to maintain quality control in production batches, we began losing a great deal of money by making refunds to purchasers of flawed material.

There was also a patent infringement suit pending against another small manufacturer of contact lens material who had a patent in the area of our invention. While we were having our other problems, this suit was settled against the manufacturer and patent holder for $30,000,000. We were amazed and horrified at this patent infringement ruling. We thought that we too might be vulnerable to a lawsuit, so in 1991 we abandoned sales.

The development of a sales program for this plastic was expensive and was a lesson in (1) controlling manufacturing and (2) making sure the title to a patent is clear and not infringing on any other patent. I will never again agree to merely a marketing license, because if I can't control the manufacturing and something goes wrong, I'm in big trouble. Also, I now do a much more thorough patent search. I won't buy or develop any technology with the slightest sign of unclear ownership or potential infringement.

Despite this setback, I decided to develop other polymer products and take the company "public" to finance sales and US Food and Drug Administration (FDA) approval costs. When the company went public, I was required to assign my invention and the other technology to the new company. I did not get any up-front payment because the underwriter of the public offering was already financing the company of which I retained an equity share.

Assignment of technology is common practice when a company goes public, and I do draw a royalty on the sales of the product for the life of my patent or twenty years, whichever comes first. The products from my polymer-based invention have gotten FDA approval and are on the market generating royalty for me. I am also still a major stockholder of the company, though I am no longer active in management.

Over the past fifteen years, I have acquired or developed more than forty patents and technology. I have licensed technology in the US, the UK, Japan, and elsewhere in Asia, and I have started five companies. This experience has been financially rewarding, but it also has provided an expensive education. I hope you can benefit from my successes and my mistakes and save yourself a lot of time, effort, grief, and expense.

Robert Hodam

# Chapter One

## Inventors' Delusions and the Realities of Profiting from Your Patent

Inventors are some of the most brilliant and creative people on the planet, but they usually have a different view of the world than do prospective buyers of their technology. Consequently, one of the most useful things I can do for other inventors is to help them see the world through the eyes of the buyer. It is important to realize there is only one reality—the reality of the person who licenses or buys your technology. (Note: In this book, I refer to licenses and assignees as the "buyers.")

It doesn't matter a bit if the buyers' viewpoints don't make sense to you; the reality is that they have the money, and unless you satisfy their needs, they are not going to give you any money. They have the gold; they make the rules. That is the reality.

In my experience, few inventors really understand the buyer, or how the invention fits into a larger picture of the market, or the expense and risk undertaken by the buyer to develop the invention into a commercial product. The different logic applied by the inventor and by the buyer to the world around them is based on experiences as different as those of Arabs and Eskimos. Assumptions that derive from these different views of the world make for many expensive misunderstandings.

For example, in one negotiation I had, the inventor was with me at a meeting with a prospective buyer. During the meeting, the inventor revealed to the prospective buyer that he had developed many important inventions in his area of expertise, in addition to the one we were proposing to sell. He went on to say that some of these inventions were even better than the one we were offering to sell.

This was an attempt on the part of the inventor to impress the prospective buyer with his expertise, hoping this might help close this deal. The prospective buyer, however, saw the inventor with suspicion—possibly as one who might be selling them something second-rate and withholding a better technology . . . and possibly one who might sell better technologies to a competing company. The deal began to go sour. The inventor was amazed when the prospective buyer became suspicious; he had difficulty seeing how his comments threatened the buyer.

This kind of misunderstanding is common and one of the main reasons why deals don't go through. Not understanding buyer behavior explains the classic case of the inventor with eighty-five patents who hasn't made a dime from any of them.

In the next sections, I describe the most common "lapses of reality" suffered by inventors with whom I have worked.

## Myopic Mania

Some inventors have trouble seeing that despite how clever and ingenious their invention is, there might be other ways to solve the problem than their invention. I once worked with an inventor of a chrome recovery device who was sure he had developed the most efficient way to recover and recycle chrome. He was right. Nothing I or the potential buyer had ever seen compared with the efficiency and low cost.

His invention was clearly the best solution to the problem of chrome recovery. However, as the price of chrome climbed, the inventor became convinced that the world would come to a stop without his invention. He refused a good offer from a major corporation because he thought he could hold out for more money.

Six months later, General Motors (GM) announced its first car model with plastic bumpers. GM had solved the problem of expensive chrome—no chrome! The price of chrome collapsed, and his invention was worthless. He missed his window of opportunity because he could not see there was always another and—if you wait long enough—a better way to solve any problem.

## Galloping Grandiosity

This is probably the most common "psychosis" of inventors. They grossly overestimate the worth of their technology and underestimate the cost and risk to the buyer of converting their invention to a product—design, testing, permits, advertising, project management, marketing, and sales expense.

For example, the cost to develop a new drug or a new chemical into a commercial product can take tens of millions of dollars of testing for the FDA and/or the US Environmental Protection Agency (EPA) and many years of processing applications and clinical trials. Even the chemical process equipment I licensed will take several million dollars to build, test prototypes. and obtain permits, not to mention the costs of marketing. (Software for nonmedical uses does not take as long or usually cost as much, but still the costs and risks are significant.)

Consequently, when many inventors get an offer for their invention, they are often tremendously disappointed by what is usually a fair and reasonable offer. I was once contacted by an inventor asking me for $20 million in exchange for 5 percent of a company to manufacture his invention.

"What company?" I inquired.

"The company I will start if you give me $20 million," he replied.

He wanted money to manufacture his patented invention, a valve to pass grit around a pump. I described to him how technologies are valued (see Chapter Three), but he was adamant that the price was $20 million and not a cent less.

"I know what it's worth," he insisted.

I got a call from an associate who said he had been contacted by a man seeking $20 million for 5 percent of a proposed company to make a patented valve. Yes, it was the same guy. I had not spoken to this inventor for seven years, and he has only three years left on his patent.

Unfortunately, someone else will soon make and sell his invention. The sales will be legal, and he won't receive a dime. This kind of thing breaks my heart. Had he not been so grandiose and stubborn, he could have been rich by now collecting royalties from a licensee who is risking money to manufacture and sell his invention.

**Patent Paranoia**

Many inventors believe they will be "ripped off" if they try to sell their technology, so they either don't do anything or they attempt to manufacture the product of their invention themselves. I can't say people haven't been ripped off, but I've never known of a case personally.

Your best friend is a good law firm specializing in intellectual property—patents, license, and technology-transfer negotiations. Your worst enemy is often yourself. Through poor preparation, it is usually the inventors who rip themselves off. What you own is intellectual property and a good attorney[1] to protect that is worth every penny you will pay.

---

[1] Get an attorney specializing in intellectual property with at least ten years of experience. A general-purpose attorney is worse than none at all in this regard. Ask for a list of clients you can contact regarding work done by the attorney. The

I worked with a nice group of inventors who sold me a technology but did not disclose to me improvements they had made on this technology. They intended to come back later and sell the improvements to me for a much greater sum. Unfortunately, they never consulted an attorney about this strategy. If they had, they would have learned that all derivative technology is part of the original technology sale. The improvements, unfortunately for them, belonged to me.

By not seeking the advice of a good intellectual property attorney, they had unwittingly given up rights to valuable improvements. I volunteered to triple their royalty and we redrafted our agreement, but with most typical buyers they would not have any legal basis for complaint.

If a corporate buyer had refused to renegotiate their agreement, would you say they were ripped off, or did they rip themselves off by not consulting an intellectual property attorney before they sold the original technology?

Read your agreement carefully and know what the words mean. In this case, the agreement clearly stated that derivative technology belonged to me, which is usually the case unless explicit exceptions are made in the agreement.

---

attorney should be part of a large law firm specializing in intellectual property or should have served an apprenticeship in one for some years. It helps if he/she is familiar with the industry that will use your invention.

There are both patent attorneys and "deal doer" attorneys among intellectual property attorneys. The patent attorney *must* know the technical area of your invention. If you are copyrighting software, the patent attorney should be an electrical engineer or a computer science graduate. If the area of your invention is biotech, then the attorney should have at least a degree in biochemistry or some biological science. Advanced degrees are preferred. The deal-doer attorneys are usually those who specialize in preparing license agreements in your field of invention. In my experience, you will need both. Again, ask for client references.

## The "I'll Make It Myself" Syndrome

Inventors occasionally believe the best option is to manufacture their invention themselves. This is sometimes valid, but not usually. Manufacturing is capital intensive. A start-up company that proposes to manufacture by buying production equipment is difficult to finance and is full of risk, management problems, and regulatory headaches.

It is usually best to contract out the manufacturing. Let others suffer the headaches and risks; they can usually manufacture it cheaper anyway. Exceptions would include products that are manufactured and sold in milligram quantities, such as research chemicals. In these cases, the value added is in the manufacturing, so you don't have much choice.

Most manufacturing is too expensive and complex for many start-ups; leave it to those who are experienced. For example, I know a doctor who invented a simple injection-molded medical device. He tried to obtain financing for injection-molding machines so he could manufacture the device himself. He tried for years to find investors, with no success.

I recommended that if he insisted on developing the product himself, he should at least contract out the injection molding, which he eventually did. He has been marketing his devices for more than five years and called to say he had decided that the hassles of regulatory compliance, workers' compensation insurance, and weak sales from underbudgeted marketing had convinced him to license the device to a major medical-device manufacturer and go back to inventing, which is what he does best.

# Chapter Two

## What Do You Actually Own?

You can't sell what you don't own. Many inventors do not have clear and exclusive title to their inventions. As part of either a license or agreement, the inventor will be asked to give warranties or indemnities relating to his owning the intellectual property of the invention. This must be done carefully, because there are significant exposures in the litigation-prone technology business.

My first "rule of invention" is that it is never too soon to see an attorney, but often too late. I have learned the hard way. As soon as I come up with what I think is likely to be a patentable or copyrightable idea, the first person I see is my attorney.

I am not especially fond of attorneys as a group. I am certainly not endorsing all aspects of the legal profession, but they are indispensable when it comes to intellectual property protection. They are my largest single business expense but worth every dime. The trick is to find a good one. I discuss this more later.

If you invent something, or even begin the process while working for someone else, you should know that most corporations, institutions of higher education, and government entities have some intellectual property policy in their employee agreements. It is critical that you review your employment agreement and company policy manuals with a good intellectual property attorney.

Even if you have been retired from the company for years or left the company years ago to work on your invention, this does not mean you are the owner of an invention even after you left employment. What the employment agreement and the policy manual of the organization that employed you says is the only thing that matters. Sometimes their claim on your invention can last for a considerable time after employment; this varies from state to state.

Of course, if you are the inventor, you are named on the patent or copyright, but that does not mean you own all rights to it. There is also a place on the patent application for designating an "assignee." The assignee could be your employer or the entity who paid for your research.

Furthermore, simply because the patent issues with only your name on it, without any designated assignee, does not mean that you own the invention. Others might claim they financially assisted with the development and therefore own the invention or they might claim they actually thought of it first.

I personally have had the experience where a claim was made that free space given me in a workshop constituted ownership because they, in effect, "financed" the development of an invention by providing free space in lieu of rent.

I have experienced two cases where someone showed up claiming to be an additional inventor. In one case, the person claimed he suggested the idea to me over coffee one day. In the other case, the guy was a former coworker with the inventor. He claimed that because he was named on the "prior art,"[2] he was party to the research leading to new claims, even though he and the inventor had not seen each other in fifteen years. Fortunately for me, in neither of these cases did the claimant prevail.

You *probably* do own "your" invention if (1) you worked on it away from company premises, (2) you did the work on your own time, (3) it is not in the scope of your employment, (4) it does not relate to the business of your employer, and (5) it is not related to work you

---

[2] Prior art is any evidence that an invention is already known.

patented or copyrighted while you were employed. But even if all these tests are true in your case, it does not guarantee you own anything.

Please consult an attorney regarding this issue before you spend a great deal of time and money trying to sell your invention, because an experienced buyer of technology will want confirmation from your employer. You will look credible to a buyer if you have obtained from your former employer a release of its claim to your invention.

I worked with one group of engineers who had developed a water treatment technology while they were employees of an aerospace company. The company, even though it was in the aerospace industry, paid their salary for several years to develop the water treatment technology and filed patents, which were subsequently issued. In fact, the company continued to pay the salaries of these researchers to continue work on water treatment for several years after the original patents were issued.

Eventually, the company lost interest and did not file patents on the research done subsequent to the patent filing. Clearly the company owned this technology, and the inventors did not contest that. However, the company abandoned efforts to commercialize this technology, and the inventors soon retired. Once retired, they renewed their interest in the technology and developed the technology beyond the original patents, which had subsequently expired.

Now, does their employer have any claim to the technology? The researchers claimed they did the work at their own lab after they retired, but how can one determine whether the work they did after retirement was really only a continuation of research done for their employer that was never patented, or whether this was really new material? They also pointed out the technology was not of interest to the company, because it was not the company's main business. But certainly for a few years the company was interested in this technology when it was paying them to research it.

Before I bought this technology, I asked the chief counsel for the company to provide me a letter abandoning any claim to the technology. The company management met and discussed whether to provide such a letter—after all, there was little incentive for them to cooperate, as they had nothing to gain and possibly something to lose.

Fortunately, my attorneys were able to persuade them to cooperate with me on abandoning their claim to the technology. When I subsequently sold the technology, the buyer insisted on a formal "quit claim" by the former employer of the inventors. Without such a letter, I could never have sold the technology.

If you have not filed a patent or copyright, you have another consideration. Are there other people who might believe they are also inventors of the technology? Consult your attorney.

In the case above, the inventors at one point disclosed that there was another person who was an inventor in the original patents, and who still lived in the area. However, they claimed he had not worked with them after they retired, and that he would say he had no claim on the current work.

How could I know that he did not think he was the inventor, and that the people I was dealing with were simply developing his idea from the time they were all employed together? I had to contact him to discuss whether the work he did when employed with the other researchers bore any resemblance to the current work. Fortunately, it did not.

Hopefully, you can see from these vignettes that the issue of ownership is always critical and usually cloudy. You cannot sell what you do not own. A buyer will need confirmation of your clear title to the product. After all, you would not buy a car without confirmation of ownership, and neither will a buyer pursue your technology without it.

# Chapter Three

## What Are Your Options?
## Licensing, Assignment, Starting Your Own Business

### What Is a License?[3]

A technology license is an agreement you use to sell to a "licensee" the rights to manufacture and/or distribute products based on your invention to someone else. It is not a transfer of ownership. A license can be either exclusive (to only one party) or nonexclusive (potentially to more than one party).

An exclusive license means that you can't exercise the license rights. The rights referred to here are those primarily for *patented* material to protect your right to make, use, and sell. Software is *copyrighted*, carrying the right to copy, distribute, and prepare derivative work, but much of the information in this book applies to it also.

It is not necessary to license the right to both manufacture and distribute, although that is the most common arrangement. It is possible to license only the right to distribute. In this case, you reserve the right to arrange manufacturing, and you sell the product to the licensee at a preset price. You can also license rights to specific geographic territories, which I will discuss later.

Common features of a license include term of agreement, geographical territory, minimum performance requirements by the licensee, support given by licensor if any, and, of course, payment amounts and schedules.

---

[3] See Sample License Agreement in Appendix.

The *term* of a license is usually at least long enough for the licensee to recover its investment (its operating and manufacturing costs plus several years of income). It might also include a provision for the licensee to extend the duration of the license, based on performance. For example, the term of a license could be twenty years on drug-related items, which require a lengthy FDA approval process, or as few as three years on software. When a patent is included in the subject matter, the term might be the life of the patent.

*Territory* describes the geographic area to which the rights are granted. Rights can be, and often are, extended worldwide when the buyer is a major international company. I do not recommend granting worldwide rights, unless the buyer is a well-established international company marketing the same type of technology as your invention.

If the licensee does not have any presence in, say, South America, consider reserving this territory for another buyer who currently has a strong presence in South America and to whom the right to manufacture is worth much more. Selling rights by territory might maximize the value to you, because the sum of the value to each licensee might be more than the value to a single licensee.

*Minimum performance* describes the specific achievements required by the licensee to continue the rights granted. This is particularly important when an exclusive license is granted. An example of specific achievements might be $0 sales in year one, $X in year two, and $XX in year three, etc. Another example might be clinical trials concluded by end of year one, FDA application filed by end of year two, initial sales by end of year five.

In drafting the minimum performance terms, the more specific and quantitative they are, the better. Also, shorter performance periods (quarterly, for example) put more pressure on a licensee to perform.

If the minimum performance is not met, then the licensee loses its rights, and you have the right to decide if you want to extend your agreement with the current licensee or find another. In the case of an exclusive license, the license might continue but not on a nonexclusive basis.

When it comes to determining whether the minimum performance is fair, put yourself in the shoes of the licensee and see if you could live with the terms you are proposing. Would you risk your money if someone offered you the same minimum performance terms?

Most licensees will expect *licensor support* in developing the technology unless all they are buying is the right to distribute. There is usually a provision in the agreement for so many "gratis" hours of your time spent in supporting a licensee who is buying the rights to manufacture. This is fair and in your best interest because you want the licensee to have a clear understanding of your product in commercially exploiting the invention.

A normal amount of gratis time could be as few as forty hours and as much as hundreds of hours, depending on the complexity of the support required. The agreement should provide you compensation on an hourly basis for any time the licensee requests beyond the gratis time. (Note: Most investors I work with underestimate the value of their time. You should charge the licensee at least as much per hour as their attorneys charge them.)

*Compensation.* This is the heart of the agreement as far as you are concerned. The description of your compensation should be quantitative, simple, and clear, consisting of two parts: (1) the up-front advance or "earnest payment" and (2) the royalty.

There should always be, in my opinion, an up-front earnest payment. I have only agreed to one license where there was nothing paid up-front. And this is the only time I have ever had a problem getting paid and getting the licensee to perform. I will never license a technology without an up-front payment again.

The agreement should expressly state whether this up-front payment is refundable or nonrefundable and whether it is a credit against recurring royalty payments. My recommendations on how to calculate up-front payment size and royalty percentage are in Chapter Four.

Some suggest that there are times when an up-front payment is not necessary, such as when the licensee is small and can't afford to pay cash. In such cases, the small company could pay in equity or pay a much higher royalty. In my experience, this is too risky. Start-up companies are inherently risky ventures that often take years to reach sales. You must be willing to wait years for any income and willing to take a chance on this company succeeding at all.

An additional problem I have encountered with granting a license to a small start-up company was recovering my technology when it filed for bankruptcy. Often the bankruptcy proceeding can tie up the ownership of your technology, and there is always the chance you could lose your technology altogether.

A payment up-front helps to ensure that the licensee is committed to developing and exploiting your technology because it has money invested. An up-front payment also tests, especially in the case of small companies, whether a licensee has the financial resources to follow-through with sales. Remember that most of these "advances" are recouped by the licensee from your royalties; that is, you get no more payments until the royalty amounts you earn pay back the advance.

The royalty is often paid on "gross sales." Royalty can also be paid on "net sales" or "profit." The problem with this is that accounting games can be played. What is "net"? How is "profit" defined? Gross sales are the easiest to quantify, but even then, the licensee might want to exclude returned product costs of coop advertising programs with retailers and promotional materials given away as samples.

I would refuse all of these exclusions to gross sales if possible because they might open the way to future disagreement. I would rather take less of a royalty percent than accept adjustments to gross sales. If the potential licensee insists on basing the royalty on net sales (deducting from gross sales certain items, such as taxes, samples, shipping, returns, etc.), discuss this with the attorney helping you with the deal and also with a good accountant, to determine which deductions can be accounted for easily.

Your attorney will know which deductions are common in the area of your invention. The critical factor is to unequivocally define the sum on which your royalty will be based. Make sure you have an inspection right to check the licensee's books and records to determine whether the right amount of royalty payment is made.

What percent of the gross sales should you propose for a royalty? The factors affecting the percentage are developed in Chapter Four. There is a psychological limit of 5 percent, which no one ventures past often, except in high-margin, high-volume, and short-term markets, such as software, which often allows at least 10 percent. Semiconductor technology allows for a 4–12 percent royalty.

But don't be too aggressive and ask for more than 5 percent unless your attorney recommends it, and only if he or she is an expert in the market for your technology and knows of recent deals done in this industry over 5 percent of gross sales.

Royalty as a percent of gross sales can go as low as 1 percent in some markets, such as the heavy equipment, electronics, and manufacturing machinery industries where often the margin is small, and the volume is low. Why? Remember, if the buyer only has a 10 percent profit on gross sales, then a 5 percent royalty on gross sales is 50 percent of the potential profit.

This does not provide much incentive for the buyer to take risks. And if there is a downturn in the market and sales drop, the profit might be zero, in which case your royalty is helping to put them out of business. The lowest royalty I have personally accepted is 2.75 percent on gross sales over $50 million. This was a heavy equipment product. All other royalties I have negotiated were 5 percent of gross sales, as defined.

If the up-front payment is an advance against royalties, you need to negotiate how much of the recurring royalty stream pays off the advance. My recommendation is for the payment to be 50 percent or less of the recurring royalties. This is discussed in more detail in Chapter Four.

## How to Decide if a License Should Be Exclusive or Nonexclusive

Usually, licenses are "exclusive," meaning no one other than the licensee will have any right to manufacture or market your invention in the specified territory. A nonexclusive license doesn't give the licensee much protection from competition, nor consequently an incentive to pay you much for the license.

You should offer exclusivity when the invention has only one application and you have a potential licensee who is dominant in the field and has worldwide sales channel. If the potential licensee markets only in the US, for instance, offer a nonexclusive license for only the territory of the US. You might separately license the foreign rights by country or region.

You should also propose a nonexclusive license when your invention has more than one application, or you could have an exclusive license within a field of use. For example, a water treatment technology could be licensed exclusively to one company for manufacture and sale only to the drinking water market for consumers, and licensed exclusively to another company for the industrial market of cooling tower water treatment.

A basic new technology for the purification of proteins produced in fermentation could be licensed to many manufacturers of protein for pharmaceutical use, giving you a royalty stream from all products manufactured using your technology. In these cases, you would likely get much more income from multiple nonexclusive licensees or exclusive licenses to a specific field of use.

## What Is an Assignment?[4]

An assignment differs from a license in one main feature—you give up all ownership of your invention. The term "full right, title, and interest" is often used to establish that you no longer own your invention and have no say whatsoever over its disposition beyond the terms of the assignment agreement. Terms of agreement, territories, minimum performance, and payment amounts and schedules differ from a license agreement.

The *term of agreement* is forever. The assignee owns your patent for all time, and it might own all derivative[5] technology too. The technology can revert to you only if the assignee breaches the agreement.

*Territory* is usually irrelevant in an assignment, but it is possible to assign by territory rather than worldwide. In an assignment, the assignee often gets all territories with the designation "full right and title." If you

---

[4] See Assignment Agreement in Appendix.
[5] Derivative is anything you ever think of related to this original invention. It is important to establish those ideas you think are *not* derivative. If you fail to establish this definition in the agreement, you will most likely have serious problems with the assignee later on about what might or might not be related, especially if you are developing similar ideas.

retain any rights at all (such as to another territory), income you get is probably not eligible for capital gains treatment. Check this with your tax advisor.

*Minimum performance* might also be irrelevant if you are paid up-front. However, if you have royalty due, then you have an interest in the assignee's performance just as with a licensee.

*Payment* is usually fairly similar to a license—an up-front payment and royalty on gross sales. As with a license, your earned royalties will go first to paying back the assignee for the advance and then they will go to you.

You should require a semiannual accounting and the right to inspect the assignee's books. The term of payment is usually twenty years or the life of the patent, whichever comes first. If it is a copyright, the term is for the life of the author plus fifty years, and a trade secret is for as long as it is secret.

### What Are the Pros and Cons of a License versus an Agreement?

A license has the advantage of you retaining the ownership and control of your technology. A license is used primarily when you wish to sell territories separately, or when you wish to manufacture and sell the product of your invention to a licensee to whom you have extended distribution rights. If the licensee doesn't perform according to the minimum performance, you can take back all rights of use.

On the other hand, you did not sell your technology just to get it back. Go into a transaction with the idea that your objective is profit, which does not necessarily require control. How is retaining ownership putting more money in your pocket?

Retaining ownership might make me feel more comfortable knowing I have not lost control, but it doesn't mean it will make me any more money than an assignment. Whether I make more money depends on the deal.

For example, an assignee will often be willing to pay more up-front advance for the full ownership conveyed in an assignment than for the more limited use provided with a license which can be revoked. *Remember,* up-front money is the best kind; royalty is always more speculative.

Another advantage of an assignment is that your income is usually taxed as capital gains because you surrender "full right, title, and interest," similar to when you sell a house, whereas income from a license is taxed as ordinary income.

The lower tax rate of capital gains can be worth 30–50 percent more in after-tax net income. However, I strongly encourage you to have a good tax attorney review the Assignment Agreement. If you don't use the right wording, the US Internal Revenue Service (IRS) will not allow capital gains treatment of *any* income.

What if the assignee never develops and sells any product based on your invention, so you never get any royalty income? This is the reason for a substantial up-front payment. Because you have lost ownership, there is not much you can do if the assignee is not otherwise in breach of the agreement. Sometimes the assignee will agree to return ownership if it has not sold a product after several years.

Another way to handle this is for the assignee to pay you in installments as certain milestones leading to development are reached. If a milestone is not reached, the technology will revert to you. If this happens, you should consult a tax attorney regarding whether you might have to file an amended tax return on income already reported as capital gains because you are now taking back ownership.

If you have a good reason to believe a potential assignee desires to acquire your invention just to "take it off the market,"[6] then (1) insist on a license so you retain ownership; or (2) make sure that you get all your money up-front; or (3) assign your invention only with clear, unambiguous milestones so breach can be easily determined.

If you firmly believe that the buyer wants to take the product of your invention off the market, then the only safe approach is to find another buyer. If this is the only buyer you can find, you might decide to assign your invention as long as you get all your money up-front. Alternatively, you could license it with tight performance requirements. Even then, it will probably cost you time and legal fees to get clear title to start over again. There is nothing like money in the bank.

I assigned a technology to a major international corporation that agreed to pay in milestones. It knew during the negotiations that certain milestones would require many years to satisfy because it had just completed the same required regulatory permit process with the same government agency on a different technology. However, this corporation led me to believe the approval process would take only a few months. It did not disclose information about the length of the permit process, which materially affects getting paid in the timeframe represented.

Can I recover the technology? Do I want the technology back? Even though the technology is assigned, and title has been transferred, payment was not complete. Therefore, the corporation breached the agreement through failure to disclose information that materially affects payment, so I can recover the technology or insist on being paid as originally agreed. In this case, I prefer to re-establish payment as originally negotiated rather than recover the technology, because the

---

[6] This often happens in the pesticide biotechnology, chemical, and pharmaceutical industries.

buyer has a huge market for this technology, and I stand to get a substantial royalty.

## What Are the Pros and Cons of Manufacturing the Product of Your Invention Yourself?

Manufacturing usually requires large amounts of planning, capital, and time. Money is hard to raise, and I can guarantee that investors will ask you why you want "capitalize" manufacturing, because most tasks can be contracted out or "outsourced." It really doesn't make economic sense to manufacture products when you can have them manufactured by contractors for far less money and effort; you will have a hard time convincing investors to the contrary. Investors will listen to a plan about contract manufacturing, or final assembly of subcontracted components, or final packaging, but not usually about manufacturing.

Another consideration in manufacturing is government regulation— workers' compensation insurance, the US Occupational Safety and Health Administration (OSHA), the EPA, the FDA, the US Federal Communications Commission (FCC), and others. Regulation is expensive because it causes delays in sales and occupies people. Why suffer this aggravation?

Yes, another consideration is employees. The administration of employees is especially difficult for small businesses that must contend with most of the same governmental hiring and firing regulations imposed on larger businesses with the personalities and personal problems inherent in any workforce. But in small businesses, there is no money for a personnel manager who can devote time to these issues. Consequently, it becomes your job to do; and that means you are spending less time on research or sales. This can be especially frustrating for an inventor unless you also enjoy managing people as much as inventing.

# Chapter Four

## How to Start Your Own Company[7]

This is the subject of an entire other book or even a set of them. I cannot possibly go into everything you should know here, so this chapter will merely raise a few key points for you to think about.

### Step One: File Patents

The most important thing you will do is to secure your intellectual property. If you mess this up, your invention is virtually worthless. Your intellectual property (copyright, patent, trade secrets, etc.) is what you have for sale. You must establish ownership. You can't sell what you don't own. You don't have to have an issued patent; an application is enough to define what you claim to own.

Always insist on a *signed* nondisclosure agreement, reviewed by your attorney before you speak to anyone. I met with an inventor of a new spark plug that offers lower emissions. He did not ask me for a nondisclosure, so I asked whether he had filed patents. He "started to" but never finished the process. I asked how long ago he first demonstrated this spark plug to anyone else. "About two years."

The one-year window of opportunity to file an application for patent after making public disclosure has probably expired, so now he can't file. He also can't confirm whether he has nondisclosure agreements with everyone he talked to about the spark plug. Consequently, there's no way to determine whether or not his technology is protected.

Unfortunately, in his enthusiasm to show his invention to investors, and in his reluctance to spend the money to protect his property, this fellow has probably lost his invention. He now owns nothing to sell.

---

[7] This chapter is largely contributed by Edward T. Engle Jr., the initial editor of this book.

## Step Two: Find the Best Management Team Possible

*This is the most important step in forming your own company!*

Employees are the most important part of any business. A good team of people can make a profit selling ice cubes in Antarctica; the wrong people can't give away gold. Investors will look first at the people, then at the technology. I don't care if you have invented the perpetual motion machine, you won't get financing without the right team. One inexpensive approach is to invite the investors to recruit a management team or at least assist you.

One other point about personnel, and this is touchy, is that you probably are not the best person for the job of president. Unless you have a great deal of experience managing one or more successful startup companies in the same industry and have a business degree from a top-notch school, don't assume that you are the best person for the job of running this company. The investors certainly won't.

There are people in any industry who do have these credentials. The investors will want these people to manage their investments. And quite frankly, so do you, because the chances of being successful and making money are probably better with an experienced person managing the operations. You could still work in the company but in a capacity more suited to your background, skills, and interests.

## Step Three: Develop a Business Plan

Don't do anything without a business plan. Investors will insist on a good plan and expect you to follow it. I think the plan should come after the team is selected, although some people draft the plan first. If you have your team selected, they can draft the portion of the plan that affects them. The new marketing manager or chief financial officer will do a better job of writing the marketing section and financials than you will; and because it is their plan, they will enthusiastically support it. There are dozens of excellent business plans found online, so I am not including one here. Even if you don't plan to manufacture your invention, prepare a business plan to develop specifics of the market for potential buyers or licensees before you begin negotiations.

## Step Four: Secure Financing

Remember the "two–three" rule. It usually takes two times as long as you anticipate to secure your financing and three times as long to reach break-even.

Money is always a key issue, maybe *the* critical issue, in any entrepreneurial activity, especially starting a manufacturing operation. The amount you need depends not only on costs specific to the technology you have developed—and the materials, personnel, and equipment to produce, warehouse, and distribute it—but also how much of the process you are funding. Are you going it alone or seeking a partner at some point? In either case, you'll need start-up capital.

Most entrepreneurs start with their own financial resources first. Unless you incorporate, you would be a sole proprietorship, and here you use your savings, home equity loans, borrowings against insurance policies, *secured* loans from banks, and the like. (*Remember:* Banks are not in the business of financing unsecured start-up ventures. They like at least three years of profitable operations before they will extend a loan; they do not want to have to run your manufacturing operation if you cannot pay the principal and interest from cash flow.)

If you need additional money, you might interest friends, coworkers, or relatives to loan you some money (always have a signed agreement!) to form a partnership (general or limited) with you or—if you are incorporated (C corporation, S corporation, or limited liability company)—to own stock in your company. Retain an attorney to advise you about the advantages and disadvantages of each option.

Another potential source of cash is a venture "angel" or private investor; attorneys, bankers, and accountants often know people interested in investing in new products, and many of these private investors advertise in local newspapers and the financial press.

Finally, you might qualify for a loan from the US Small Business Administration (SBA) or a US Small Business Investment Company (SBIC) investment. Check with your local bank for those near you.

There are other ways to obtain start-up capital, but they are less often used. They include commercial finance companies, suppliers who extend trade credit, inventory lenders, accounts receivable financiers (factors), borrowing against future purchase orders, or leasing assets that have a substantial, easily defined value.

If you need large sums of money or if you plan on manufacturing your technology entirely yourself instead of simply developing it to a certain point and then licensing or assigning it to someone else, then you will require (substantial) additional capital. Private investors might be a source, or it might be time to approach a venture capital (VC) firm.

However, by far the vast majority of start-ups are financed by private investors. In either case, *you must have a detailed business plan*. VCs have little interest in companies that are only developing one or two products. Instead, they look for a series of products or at least the seeds of a series.

In addition, most VCs do not invest sums less than $2 million, so don't waste your time if you need "only" $300,000. Unless you are an experienced entrepreneur, more complex methods of raising money, such as "going public," might not be open to you.

All VCs and private investors look for superior management skills, extraordinary technology capabilities, sustainable barriers to entry by others, and proprietary technology or processes. Although they sometimes form partnerships with technology developers, usually they will take an equity position in your company (thus, you must be incorporated) or receive "convertible debt"—a loan that can be converted to stock at their discretion.

A final funding suggestion is that for the right kind of product, you might find an existing corporate sponsor in your field to help capitalize it as a subsidiary or a joint venture.

If you get through step four, you are 50 percent of the way to success. Good luck!

# Chapter Five

## How to Estimate the Value of Your Invention

Estimating the value of your invention is part science and part art, and the formula differs depending on whether you license or assign your technology. In this chapter is a step-by-step description of a fairly quantitative process I use to estimate the value of a patent or technology.

The basic concept is simple. Buyers are not going to pay you more than they expect in profits (revenues less costs). In fact, buyers will pay you a small percent of the "present value" of the income stream they expect to get from selling the product developed from your invention. Usually the buyers will pay, in some combination of up-front payment and recurring royalty payment, no more than 25 percent of the present value of what they perceive is likely to be their profit over time.

It is important to remember this concept when developing estimates. Put yourself in the position of buyers. Would you risk your money and time, as they will have to do, to turn your invention into a product for a profit of less than 75 percent of your normal profit? Because the payment to you is usually based on a percent of gross sales, if the buyers' profit is smaller than expected, they might have almost no interest in developing your product because they can make more profit doing something else.

For example, if the royalty is set at 5 percent of gross sales, and the buyers' profit is normally 20 percent of gross sales, you would be receiving 25 percent of the expected profits (5%/20% = 25%). If the buyers' profit on gross sales is only 10 percent, a royalty of 5 percent of gross sales equals 50 percent of the buyer's profit! They will not agree to this percent of royalty on gross sales, and neither would you, because there are many low-risk investments one can make to turn a 5 percent profit. Ask yourself what would motivate you to accept your own proposal if the situation were reversed.

### How to Estimate the Value of an Assignment of Your Patent to a Buyer

The first thing you must do is to make a realistic assessment of the potential sales for the patent buyer. Conduct some market research to estimate the maximum sales possible.

For example, if your invention reduces pollution from cars, then the buyer of your technology cannot possibly sell more units than there are cars in which to put them. The number of cars manufactured is the maximum number of sales physically possible, or *total theoretical market* (TTM).

This sets the upper boundaries of the sales universe, but not the upper boundary of realistic sales. Realistically, the sales will be much less than this number because it is simply never possible to sell one of anything to everyone who wants or needs one, even when required by law. It just doesn't happen.

Next, estimate the *realistic market share* (RMS). Using the same example, subtract the cars that will use some other means of controlling pollution (there will always be some other way to meet air emission standards. Remember the chrome recovery example in Chapter One).

A good rule of thumb for the RMS is 5–10 percent of the TTM, because history shows that, on average, successful products can be expected to have market penetration in this range. They can occasionally get much more, but for the purpose of estimating a realistic, conservative number on which to base a value, this is a good range.

If you have independent market research that suggests a larger percentage is defensible, then by all means use that number. Just remember that you will have to defend it to a patent buyer.

Then estimate your buyer's *cost of manufacturing* (COM) your product. These costs are often referred to as "variable costs," because they vary with the quantity of products manufactured. If you are not familiar with the kind of manufacturing necessary to make a product from your invention, ask someone who manufactures a similar product for an estimate. You might also ask faculty members of the Industrial Engineering Department of any major university for an estimate.

Next, add to the COM, the buyer's *cost of sales* (COS), which are the buyer's administrative overhead, salaries, legal fees, rent, sales and promotion expenses, etc., *that pertain to this product* regardless of the number of units manufactured or sold (this is often called the "fixed cost"). This varies widely by industry, but the COS can often be estimated as a function of COM.

Here are some rough guidelines.

- Electronic and mechanical industrial devices: COS equals the COM.
- Pharmaceutical and over-the-counter drug products: COS equals five to eight times the COM, including the expense of FDA approval and research and development (R&D).
- Software: COS equals five to eight times the COM.
- Consumer electronics: COS equals two to three times the COM.

Now, estimate the likely price the buyer of your technology will charge his or her distributors for the product resulting from your invention. *Buyer's price* (BP) can probably be estimated from the wholesale price of a similar item. Check the list price in stores and catalogs (the retail price), then divide the list price in half for an estimate of your buyer's likely wholesale price. (The markup from manufacturer to distributor to retailer is not always 100 percent, but that would not be uncommon.)

Please note that the BP is *not* the price the buyer charges for a product that incorporates your invention but applies only to the part of the product that *is* your invention.

For example, suppose you have invented a new valve to bypass grit around pumps, and you sell this valve to a pump manufacturer. If the buyer-manufacturer doesn't sell your technology as a stand-alone product but as a component of some of its existing pumps, there is no BP per se, because there is no unit sold. Therefore, you should estimate the added value of your valve to the pump manufacturer.

Your technology is not worth 5 percent of the gross sales of a pump in which it is incorporated if the manufacturer was selling those pumps anyway. The buyer-manufacturer of your valve might, however, enjoy increased sales of this revised pump.

Your payment should be based on the *increment of increased sales,* because that is the benefit to your buyer. If the buyer's sales of a particular pump go from $1 million to $2 million, all other costs being equal, you should get a percentage of this incremental $1 million increase. The percentage to which you are entitled can be estimated in the same way as any other royalty as shown later in this chapter.

Also, consider the trend in mass markets toward decreasing prices over time. This is the case in consumer electronics and software, for example. You might need to allow for the fact that the BP will decrease over time and use an average price over the life of the product for the BP.

Next, estimate the likely *life of market* (LOM) for your product. Some products, like software, last only a few years in the market before being replaced by a better version, but industrial processes can last for decades. Most consumer products are good for five to ten years. Drugs and over-the-counter products can last for the life of the patent but often are for a shorter time. Of course, the shorter the market life, the smaller the sales and the smaller your payment.

Next, estimate the *ramp-up time* (RUT). Your buyer will also require a period of time to develop your invention into a product. The buyer will, during this period, incur certain costs of development, which convert your invention to a product. (I've never seen an invention that was ready to sell, an invention that was already a "product" the buyer did not have to risk any money on to test or permit or package.)

The buyer's cost of development includes market research, package design, field testing, permitting, and perhaps government approvals. These product developments take RUT. For software, consumer electronics, industrial processes and devices, and other technology that do not usually require government approval, RUT can be a year or more. During this time, there are no sales, only expenses. The marketing department of a major university business school will be able to help estimate the RUT required for your type of product.

Once sales start, there is a *penetration rate* (PR). This is the number of years in which the market accepts the product to the fullest extent possible. Penetration rate varies widely by industry; but for a rough estimate, assume the rate is linear and takes two years at least to reach the projected market share for fast turn-over items, like software, and three to seven years for consumer goods.

For the first year of market penetration, set year one sales equal to zero. There often are sales, but for our purposes you can ignore them. Determine the last year of penetration by a leveling in the slope of the curve plotting sales over time. Once the slope changes, the full market share is reached. Again, the marketing department of a major university business school might help with such estimates.

Bringing the above definition together, my formula to estimate the profit of the buyer is as follows.

### Estimated Profit to the Buyer Each Year

TTM =          Total Theoretical Market (units/year)

RMS =          Realistic Market Share (%)

COM =          Cost of Manufacturing ($/unit)

COS =          Cost of Sales ($/unit)

BP =           Buyer's Price ($/unit)

LOM =          Life of Market (years)

RUT =          Ramp-Up Time (years)

PR =           Penetration Rate (years)

$$Z \text{ (buyer's profit per year)} = [(TTM \times RMS) \times (BP-COM-COS)]$$

This formula works for any technology that is turning over annually and you have figures for current annual sales of similar products. For example, if you have developed some new source code and you know the annual units of software now sold to which your code applies (TTM), the above formula works. Or, for example, your technology is side-door air bags and you know the number of cars sold per year (TTM), then this formula will also give you the *buyer's profit per year.*

On the other hand, if you have a retrofit market or your technology is applicable to a fixed set of existing sites, such as sulfur scrubbing technology for the stack gas emissions of power plants or a new asphalt recovery technology, then the formula needs to be modified. In these cases, there are a known and fixed set of sites where your technology applies, and in the life of the technology there will not be substantial increases.

Therefore, you must take this fixed TTM and divide it by the years of LOM, less the RUT and less the average time for a PR to reach the RMS. Therefore,

Z (buyer's profit per year for a fixed number of sales) =

$$\frac{[(TTM \times RMS) \times (BP\text{-}COM\text{-}COS)]}{(LOM\text{-}RUT\text{-}1/2PR)}$$

The last step in estimating the reasonable size of your payment is to estimate *present value* (PV), also known as present worth. You probably had this concept explained in an economics course or explained in the back of finance, accounting, chemistry, or physics book, but the basic concept is simple. Money is worth more now than later, and future sums are therefore discounted.

A formula for calculating PV is shown below. PV is important because if you are expecting to be paid now, in today's dollars, then you will be paid a fraction of the PV of the future income stream to the buyer from your product (its PV).

Calculate the PV of the above buyer's profit (Z) using the following formula.

**Present Value of the Buyer's Estimated Profit Per Year**

$$PV = Z \times \frac{(1 - 1/(1 + i)^n)}{i}$$

- PV equals the total value in today's dollars of the buyer's estimated profit in an average year during the LOM.
- Z is the estimated annual profit of the profit calculated above.
- "i" is an estimated interest rate equal to the cost of money during the LOM.
- "n" is the time period or LOM.

The present value of 100 percent of the *projected* PV is all your invention is worth to buyers today. If they risk money now, this is the most they can hope to make in today's values.

If everything in product development goes well and there is no risk that this profit will be realized, the buyer would be willing to pay you no more than, say, 25 percent of this number. Why should the buyer do this? You wouldn't. But there *is* risk, so the buyer will usually not pay more than 20 percent of the PV of the estimated profit.

### How to Estimate the Total You Can Expect to Get Paid for an Assignment of Your Technology

Twenty percent of the PV of all the projected buyer's profit is what I call *reasonable total value* (RTV). Because 20 percent of buyer's profit is not too unreasonable a price for you to ask a buyer as some combination of up-front advance and royalty.

$$RTV = 0.2 \times PV$$

Twenty-five percent of PV is probably the maximum you can reasonably ask, but only if the buyer can expect million in sales within six months.

### How to Estimate What You Can Get Paid Up-Front

Fifty percent of the RTV (10 percent of the projected buyer's profit) paid up-front is high. Twenty percent of the RTV (4 percent of the buyer's profit) paid up-front is reasonable, but you can't expect to get much more. A typical division between up-front advance and royalty on gross sales looks like this.

| | |
|---|---|
| Up-front payment = | 0.2 RTV |
| Royalty on gross sales = | 0.8 RTV |
| Total income = | 1.0 RTV |

If you want to be cashed out up-front, with no royalty on sales, then 30–50 percent of a 20 percent RTV is probably the maximum amount you should ask for, because you are asking the buyer to take 100 percent of the risk. To get as much as 50 percent of a 20 percent RTV up-front (10 percent of the buyer's estimated profit), you will have to reduce the risk to the buyer to almost zero.

Reality check. If your calculation of the up-front value to you is in the tens of millions, check your numbers. Something is probably wrong. The largest up-front payment in which I have been involved is $26 million, paid by one corporation to another corporation for a fully developed core technology of copying machines. But payments of this size are unusual. Mid-seven-figure, up-front payments are uncommon, but $1 million up-front payments are common when the risk is low, and/or the payoff to the buyer is huge.

Before we discuss the royalty computation, let me suggest a method to increase the accuracy of your estimate of the buyer's profit. Ask the buyer. Once you have done your homework and generated your own estimates, ask for a meeting with the buyer in which you present each assumption, one at a time, and allow him or her to react.

While most (not all) companies routinely go through this process internally to estimate the price they are willing to pay for a technology, they won't expect an inventor to be this sophisticated. They will be impressed that an inventor has taken the time to make realistic estimates and is being so reasonable. They will also find it difficult to argue with good quantitative estimates.

I learned this method of joint valuation during a negotiation in Japan over the license of robotics device. The potential licensees sat down and went through their calculations of the value of the proposed technology. I had a chance to correct false assumptions and comment if I thought a certain number was too high or too low. They allowed me to participate in the process of arriving at each number.

This removed all sense of arbitrariness to analyzing the numbers. I knew where each number came from, the method used to calculate the value, and all assumptions that went into the calculations. Once I agreed that the individual numbers were fair and reasonable, arguing with the final value was difficult because it was derived by simple arithmetic.

I find this approach greatly reduces later disagreement over the value. Joint valuation prevents you from having unrealistic expectations and forces the buyers to be reasonable too. I have had great success with this approach, and I usually get good cooperation from the buyer in developing the estimates because they too want to know what my technology is worth.

Install the above formula into a spreadsheet software program. Take a laptop computer and your spreadsheet model to a meeting with the buyer set up specifically to discuss the value of the technology. As values for each parameter are agreed to, insert them into the model in the computer. Because you already should have your own numbers based on your research, you will know as you go along whether the buyer's assumptions are far from your own.

Reach agreement on values for each parameter one at a time during the meeting. This process will, of course, instantly produce a present value of the buyer's expected profit at the end of the meeting for all to consider and react on the spot.

Occasionally, I have encountered a company that will agree with the numbers as they were being generated but balk when they were totaled. When this happens, you might want to consider another buyer, because this one is not too cooperative. More about buyers is discussed in Chapters Six and Seven.

## How to Estimate Your Royalty Percentage

The royalty is paid in the future, so the estimation of actual dollar amounts is in future dollars, whereas the up-front payment is calculated in present dollars. The percentage, however, can be calculated in either future or present dollars because it is not an absolute amount but a percentage.

For example, using present value, if the RTV equals 20 percent of the buyer's profit (as a percent of gross sales) and royalty equals 80 percent of RTV, and if the buyer's profit margin on gross sales is 20 percent, then the royalty percent of gross sales equals 3.2 percent (80% x 20% x 20% = 3.2%).

Another example is when the RTV is equal to 25 percent of the buyer's profit of 20 percent and the royalty is 90 percent of RTV, then the royalty percent is 4.5 percent (25% x 90% x 20% = 4.5%).

On software, the example might be if the RTV is 35 percent of the buyer's profit, the buyer's profit margin is 40 percent and the royalty is 95 percent of the RTV, then the percentage is 12 percent (0.35 x 0.40 x 0.95%). A royalty this high is possible because the risk is relatively low, and the sales are near term.

This classic royalty of 5 percent of gross sales is derived from an RTV of 25 percent on a 25 percent profit on gross sales, and a royalty of 80 percent RTV equals 5 percent (25% x 25% x 80% = 5%).

## How to Estimate the Value of a License; Up-Front, Royalty

Remember, a license is different from an assignment in that ownership does not transfer. With a license, the owner of the patent/technology (the licensor) retains ownership. The holder of the license (licensee) only has the right to use the patent/technology for some specified period in a specified territory and perhaps for a limited purpose. The terms of a license agreement were disclosed in Chapter Three, but they are repeated here because they affect the value of the license.

The first rule of thumb is that a license is worth less than an assignment by virtue of the simple fact that the ownership does not transfer. Therefore, a licensee can be expected to pay less. Think of it as buying a house (assignment of title) versus renting a house (a license to use it). If you are buying, you pay up-front. If you are renting, you pay first and last month's rent, or maybe you only pay the rent as you go. It is much the same thing in licensing. Do not expect the licensee to pay much, if anything, up-front.

However, the more rights you grant to the licensee, the more commitment the licensee can be expected to offer. For example, a licensee will pay more for a ten-year license than a three-year license with a renewal clause. A licensee might be willing to pay more if a broader territory is granted; for instance, worldwide rights rather than US rights. Conversely, the more stringent you make the minimum performance conditions, the greater the risk to the licensee of losing the license; and therefore, the less he or she might be willing to pay.

The royalty percentage should be the same as an assignment, but the front-end payment, sometimes called an "earnest payment," is probably less than 5 percent of the calculated front-end payment for an assignment. You should ask for some up-front payment just to confirm that the licensee is "earnest." Make the up-front payment of a license at least large enough to recoup your expenses in securing the license. Consider asking 5 percent of the estimated assignment value.

### How to Estimate the Value of
### Starting Your Own Company to Market Your Invention

This is a difficult estimation. On one hand, the potential value, on paper, of starting one's own business to manufacture and sell one's invention is far greater than either licensing or assigning your invention. On the other hand, the odds of success are small, and it will take a much longer time to realize any money from the venture. If you have correctly estimated the market and sales using the formulas in this chapter, then you know what profit you and your investors (who supply your start-up capital) could be putting into your own pockets, if successful.

One consideration is that the investors will probably end up owning the majority share, so you might get only, say, 5–10 percent of the profits, if you are lucky (rarely does anyone who starts a high-technology business end up owning more than 10 percent). In addition, you might have to wait years until the company is profitable to take out any money in an "exit strategy"—selling to another company, going public, or declaring large dividends from profit.

However, if you assign your technology, you get most of your money now and the assignee takes all the risk. Also, if you are a true inventor, you have another invention rolling around in your head. The current invention is probably not your only opportunity to develop something valuable.

My advice is to assign your invention and start to work on something new. You will be better off in the near term because you have some money in your pocket, and better off in the long term because you stand to profit both from royalties on sales and from future inventions.

# Chapter Six

## How to Increase the Value of Your Invention

In addition to the value of the profit as estimated in Chapter Four, there are several things I have done to increase my income from the sale of my technology: (1) reduce the risk to the buyer, (2) sell the technology to a buyer for equity in a new venture, and (3) offer to buy the product resulting from your technology.

### 1. Reduce the Risk to the Buyer

**Accept Up-Front Installment Payments**

The low-cost way to reduce risk to the buyer and to get an up-front payment too is to accept installment payments. I sold (assigned) a technology that had been demonstrated in a lab, and a large field prototype of it had been tested briefly. Engineering this technology into a final product will not be difficult for the buyer, but the buyer will need to get government permits; and because patents are not yet filed, patent protection is uncertain.

We agreed on a value to be paid when the risk associated with specific unknowns are eliminated. I could have applied for the patents and permits myself, which would take time and more money. I chose instead to limit my investment in this case and accept an installment payment, where the entire price is agreed to in advance, but only a small up-front payment is made on signing (10 percent of the first installment). When the patents issue, I get a fixed amount; when the permits issue, I get the balance of the first installment.

In this arrangement, I have reduced the buyer's risk because it is not obliged to pay me until the risk of permits and patents is entirely removed before it pays any substantial amount. If the permits or patents do not issue, the buyer has the option of either not paying, in which case the technology reverts to me, or paying me the balance due if the buyer wants to complete the purchase.

The kinds of risks the buyer will face include permits by government agencies, engineering scale-up and testing, manufacturing processes, patent protection, and customer acceptance. You can reduce all these risks yourself by filing for the applications and building and testing a prototype, if you have the money (no small problem).

### File a Patent Application

I suggest the least expensive and perhaps the most valuable step you can take to make a meaningful reduction in risk to the buyer is to file for patents. If you have not done this before, find a patent attorney who specializes in the field of your invention to file the application for you. You can try to write the patent description yourself, especially the "prior art" section, if you are experienced at writing patents.

The most important consideration in selecting a patent attorney is finding one who specializes in your field. I once hired a good patent law firm to write a patent for me on a drug-related product. The senior partner, a patent attorney with a degree in mechanical engineering, drafted the patent. The draft patent application was a disaster because he kept describing the devices in which the product would be used instead of the formulation. I had to take it to another firm that specialized in drugs and chemical processes and have the application completely rewritten.

You might also consider writing the entire patent yourself, including doing the patent search. There are many patent databases online.

A patent application reduces risk because it establishes a sound argument for uniqueness that will likely satisfy the IS Patent and

Trademark Office (USPTO). An application does not mean that a patent will be issued. There is still risk, but at least the buyer's patent attorney can judge the likelihood of a patent issuing that will provide valuable coverage, and the buyer can judge the risk of infringing on "prior art."

The other thing a patent application does is to define the technology. Without an application, you might encounter difficulty establishing the bounds of the technology being sold. You must be able to identify the core technology on which derivative technology claims might be based. A patent application reduces the risk of later misunderstandings about what is being sold and what is not.

## Build a Prototype

A full-scale prototype is important to reduce the risk of engineering problems in manufacturing and operation, but in some industrial processes this is expensive.

I once licensed a medical device in Japan to measure nystagmus of the eye. The inventor went with me to Tokyo and took a suitcase-sized prototype. It was crude looking, but when it was turned on and the image came up on the screen, there were "oohs" and "aahs." This deal was as good as done. I estimate that the crude-working prototype doubled our up-front payment.

I also licensed a robotics device in Japan, but I had to convince the Japanese buyer to fly to California to see the system operate. I took to Kyoto a video of the inventor's full-scale working prototype in operation, and the buyers were in California within a week. The deal successfully closed four months later.

## Ask the Prospective Buyer to Pay for the Prototype

If you can't afford to build a prototype, ask the buyer to pay for it. If the buyer is serious, the investment of, say, $20,000 might be acceptable.

I sold a chemical process technology that had to demonstrate the full process from start to finish. Only portions had been demonstrated at lab scale. The patents were based on the chemistry of certain parts of the technology but not as an integrated process.

I asked the buyer to buy the technology "as is," or, if the buyer was willing to invest $15,000 in materials, the inventor would donate his time (actually, I paid him) and set up a full process to demonstrate the entire system operating. The buyer agreed. The demonstration was a success, and I more than doubled what we[8] got up-front.

## Develop a Good Marketing Plan

Another way to increase the value to you and the perceived value to the buyer is to develop a good marketing plan. This means that you conduct research on all the possible markets and the economics, including the following information.

- An analysis of the competition, showing quantitatively why your technology is significantly more economical to use or offers significantly better quality to the consumer.

- An estimate of the market size, such as the number of units now being sold, which your invention will replace. (Substantiated sales estimates in the millions of dollars are nice, but billions are a thousand times more interesting!)

---

[8] I bought an option on the invention from the inventor, so I owed him a percent of my up-front payment and royalty.

- If your technology is to be used in a process to manufacture something else, you must show that your technology will decrease the overall costs of goods to the manufacturer by at least 50 percent.

- If your technology is to be incorporated into another product as a component, then your technology should increase the performance of the resulting product by at least 100 percent or decrease the price by 50 percent. Anything less will not be worth much.

- An analysis of the economics of your invention to show the estimated cost of goods and the profitability of the products resulting from your technology (you need this to estimate the value of your sale).

- Identify the means and cost of distribution and sales.

- Written indication of interest on the part of potential buyers.

When you finish this written plan, sit down with the buyer (after the buyer has signed a nondisclosure agreement) and discuss the potential of your invention.

I realize this is beginning to sound a lot like sales, because it *is* sales. Promoting a plan to the buyer is salesmanship. It is probably distasteful to most investors, but you need to do it. "Perception is reality" in marketing. If buyers perceive that they have a huge upside potential, taking a risk is less onerous.

If you can't develop all the information, at least work out the economics of the competition and the market size. I always prepare a market analysis for every technology before I buy it, then I use the same analysis when I resell the technology.

Remember, millions of dollars in new sales might be peanuts to your buyer, so if you can make a legitimate case for *billions,* by all means, do it. But be careful that you don't overstate the market size and lose credibility. You might need to use some imagination and think of completely new applications and markets to increase the potential, but if you can justify the numbers, then use them.

## 2. Sell the Technology to a Buyer for Equity in a New Venture

Consider selling your technology to a buyer in exchange for cash and equity in a venture based on the technology. Some buyers, including me, buy technologies for a percent of the net income estimated to come to them, then start companies to use the technology with the intention of either selling the company or the fully developed technology. This way we defer our risk by not paying upon signing (I usually get twenty-four months to make the first payment), and the inventors have a larger up-side potential because they might own some equity in the company I create around their technology, in addition to their royalty.

Or, in other cases, I might simultaneously buy an existing company, manufacture the product of the invention at the new company, thus increasing the sales and value of the purchased company, then sell the company and reap the increased value.

The value to you of such arrangements is greatly increased, near-term (two to five years) income potential. Equity ownership in a company developed by a buyer can be worth many times what you could ever get merely from a royalty and up-front payment. The buyer is increasing your ultimate income by creating additional value, such as starting a business to use the invention in a product, finding buyers, financing a demonstration, or adding your technology to some other technology to form a more valuable package to a subsequent buyer.

### 3. Offer to Buy the Product Resulting from Your Technology

Another way to reduce risk to the buyer is to offer to buy back the technology's products yourself and then resell or use them. I have done this in a case where I wanted to start a company to market the technology in an application other than the one the buyer envisioned at the time of the sale. If you aren't interested in selling the product yourself, then find someone to buy it from you who will place an order pending its development.

If you don't know how or don't want to start a company, then find a customer you can introduce to the buyer of your technology. Identifying potential buyers in a new market greatly increases the value of your technology. Preproduction purchase orders would be great, but you probably won't get them. However, you can get letters expressing interest in a purchase if the invention is ever commercialized. I would estimate that this increases the interest of your buyer and your income potential by a factor of at least two, depending on various factors.

I bought a technology that I wanted to market myself, but I didn't want to use a contract manufacturer because I thought I could receive a better price for the technology if I assigned it to a company that would manufacture it for existing markets and sell me back equipment created by my technology for a new market I had developed.

Remember that I said I don't like to manufacture my products in-house, so I'm talking here about marketing—which is much less capital intensive. I would only set up the marketing and sales company, and I would not operate the company myself for long. I can make more money starting another business and letting someone else run the first one.

If you propose to the buyer of the technology to buy some of the equipment or products manufactured based on your technology, the buyer will probably feel much more comfortable because there are potential sales and income beyond the buyer's own markets. What could be better? The buyer sells the products from the purchased technology in the current market, and you propose to increase sales even more by buying the equipment yourself for your own projects.

In developing new markets for the product of my invention, I'm trying to do three things.

1. By guaranteeing purchase of the product, I increase the value of my technology to the buyer so I get a larger cash settlement up-front.

2. This speeds production and increases sales, so I make more from royalty income in the future.

3. It greatly leverages the sale of the technology for perhaps substantially more income by setting up a new company to buy and to sell the product of my own technology.

Here's a vignette that ties together several of the concepts of this chapter.

I completed the sale (assignment) of technology to a major US company that is using it in its market. I am setting up a company to market the product for other applications. When I went to the president of this company with a proposal, I had completed a full business plan, which showed the potential sales of this technology to the company's existing customers, to my potential customers, and the new market share the company would get in its market.

The company saw a detailed strategy that focused on sales and income, presented in a financial format rather than a plan that focused on the technology alone. (Remember that your audience is the president, and he or she might not be a technical person but instead focus on finance or marketing.) In fact, the plan did not even mention how the technology works. The technology was treated as if it were a black box.

Initially, the upper management of most companies doesn't care how your technology works, and you don't want to reveal too much about the details anyway. Just tell them what your technology does, quantitatively.

This particular technology had a potential billion-dollar market removing dissolved organic material from water 50 percent more cheaply than the current technology. The market size and economics were all I described, because any more technical information would have made their eyes glaze over. A corporate buyer is going to buy your technology because of the money the company might make, not because of how your technology works.

Keep in mind that the buyer of the technology ultimately is the president of the company, not the R&D guy or a senior engineer or any other technical guy. Of course, the senior technical person will be asked to evaluate your technology and make a recommendation as to whether it can be made to perform as you describe.

If that person is not able to present your technology in bottom-line terms, such as sales and profit margins that can be documented, then you are not going to get the president's attention. And if you do not get the president's attention, you will not get much, if anything, for your technology. Again, thoroughly prepare your financial projections to show the benefits to your targeted buyer.

# Chapter Seven

## How to Find a Licensee or a Buyer

This chapter describes a step-by-step method to identify potential buyers and uses an example of a project I was involved in to show how each step is taken.

### Identify Applications for Your Technology

First, identify all the possible applications for your invention. Then ask yourself what kind of company would make money manufacturing your invention in each of the industries represented. For example, I'm working with some inventors who have developed a new plastic that is twice as strong as fiberglass yet is the same weight and cost. Is this a product they sell to the chemical industry, or would an end-user, like car, aircraft, or boat manufacturers, be interested because strength-to-weight ratios are important in their products?

I believe this product is worth more to the ultimate user because they can benefit from it most; a chemical company would only sell to these people anyway. An end-user licensee, such as an auto or aircraft manufacturer, can always find an ISO 9000 (a quality management system) chemical company to manufacture this plastic for them. To a large chemical company, such a plastic would be relatively insignificant . . . just another product.

### Prioritize Applications

However, to a manufacturer who can use the plastic in their products and can double sales in only a few years, this plastic is extremely valuable. In this case, we considered the fact that the auto and aircraft manufacturers have long manufacturing lead times. They design and plan their products years in advance, and they will test components for years too. They are a market for this product eventually, but not a near-term one. Consequently, we initially focused on the small boat market.

Small boats (kayaks and canoes) do not require the long production lead time of cars and planes. Boat manufacturers will certainly test prototype boats and their materials, but they will incorporate new materials much sooner. A kayak made of Kevlar sells for three times the price of a fiberglass kayak, simply because it is as strong and half the weight. But because Kevlar is expensive for boat manufacturers to buy, its cost is passed on to the consumer in a price-competitive market.

The impact of a lightweight, inexpensive material is profound on sales of small boats that must be portaged in shallow streams and hand-carried by their owners from the vehicle to the water and back. We're not excluding the huge potential in the car market, but we're just not focusing on it right now. The largest market is not always the one to focus on first, if it will take a long time to develop. In this example, we could run out of money while waiting years for GM to test the material, but small boat manufacturers will see the largest immediate benefit with the least change to their current operations.

### Develop Multiple Licensee Options

To maximize our gain from the sale, we will provide exclusive licenses to use our plastic but only in the existing products of licensees in several distinct markets. Boat manufacturers will not be sold the right to manufacture our material—only to use it. They don't have the ability to work with chemical compounds, and this way we can control the exclusivity of our licenses because the licensee cannot sell our material to a different market where it might be used by a competitor of one of our other exclusive licensees.

We might enter into an exclusive license to manufacture with a single chemical company, but only after we have granted licenses to boat manufacturers to use the plastic. The more we can show the chemical manufacturer that it will have immediate sales, the more it is worth. The chemical manufacturer will be limited to selling only to us or to our exclusive licenses, that way we protect our licensee exclusivity from the chemical manufacturer's competition. For that protection, the license is worth more. (If we don't provide such protection, a license might not be worth anything.)

By reserving the option for us to sell plastic to our exclusive licensees directly, we have the option of becoming a supplier. We do not ever want to be the manufacturer. We can't afford the expense or hassle of becoming an ISO 9000-certified chemical manufacturer for one product. We can buy it cheaper from our exclusive chemical manufacturer licensee.

If we end up selling the plastic product to our licensees, it will be because we will not only make the royalty on the sales of the ultimate product, but we also make a profit on the sale of the raw material. We will have a small advertising and marketing cost because we would be selling to a few exclusive users. We will need a warehouse to store inventory from our chemical manufacturer, that will probably produce our entire annual sales in a batch once a year. This sales business is not labor intensive, does not require any capital investment in equipment, and has little risk once user-licensees are found.

## Identify the Territories and Applications

We plan to license a user in each distinct market and geographical territory. The first license will probably go to a large US manufacturer of small boats (market one, probably for sale in North America only, territory one). The European market will be a separate license, unless the US manufacturer markets worldwide (market one, territory two).

Then we plan to sell an exclusive license for our plastic to a large manufacturer of large power and sailboats (market two for sale in the US/Canada, territory one). We will then license to a manufacturer in Europe (territory two) and next in Australia (territory three).

The kayak and canoe market is a somewhat different market from the large powerboat and sailboat market, so there is not likely to be much overlap in application. There might be some manufacturers that can make a good case that they sell their products worldwide and should therefore be given an exclusive worldwide license. If this is the case, we will weigh the expense of finding a foreign licensee against the potential of better sales from a foreign manufacturer in the foreign market.

**Locate the Names and Addresses of Buyers**

Okay, once you decide on likely users and you select the largest near-term markets, how do you find these companies? Easy. Check ThomasNet (once known as the *Thomas Registry*). ThomasNet.com lists detailed information about suppliers, products, computer-aided design (CAD) models, diverse suppliers, and insights.

Once you have several major companies picked out, contact each one to request product literature in your area of interest and an annual report (a public company must send you one). Annual reports tell you all about a company's financial condition and might suggest whether it is expanding and acquiring new technology. The annual report's letter from the executive director or board chair to the stockholders will describe the markets the company is planning to get into and the R&D it is pursuing, in general terms.

If the company proudly reports the acquisition of new technologies, it probably has a policy of looking outside the company for new products. If it doesn't report any new product research or acquisitions, it might be either a declining business or have the deadly "not-invented-here syndrome" (NIHS).

Put these companies far down on your list of potential buyers. Also, if they have not been profitable the past two years, they likely are not in the mood to risk anything on new technology until they get their regular business on track again. Initially reject unprofitable companies.

If the company is not public, you can search Dun & Bradstreet (D&B), which provides commercial data, analytics, and insights, but it is expensive and not really necessary for every company in which you are interested. I recommend that you don't invest in a D&B report until you know for sure that you intend to contact a specific company. Even though private companies are not obliged to send you an annual report, call to ask for general company information and product literature.

## Ranking Buyers

The following is my priority ranking for possible buyers.

### Target

1. Companies that are most profitable and cash rich in dollars, not percent, like profit margins or return on equity. If they don't have any spare cash, they can't afford to pay you.

2. Companies that report new technology acquisitions in their annual reports or product literature. This indicates they have allocated money for technology acquisition, and they have a policy of buying new technologies outside the company.

3. Companies with large R&D budgets. This doesn't mean they don't have the NIHS, but at least they like new technology.

4. Companies with excellent reputations in the industry. This might suggest they will treat you fairly, and it's always better to be associated with the top companies.

5. Companies headed by an engineer or a scientist. They will have a much more positive image of inventors than most finance or marketing-type CEOs.

6. Companies with large subsidiaries of public companies might be interested in "spin-off" or going public themselves, but they don't have any new technology (check the subsidiaries owned by large public conglomerates).

### Avoid

1. Companies involved in patent infringement lawsuits. This tells me they don't have good intellectual property advice and might disregard a nondisclosure agreement.

2. Companies in bankruptcy or being acquired. Who knows if they can ever afford to develop your invention and pay you?

3. Companies involved in any kind of major lawsuit that could bankrupt the company, tarnish its reputation, or affect sales.

4. Companies without human resources and money to adequately market your product.

# Chapter Eight

## How to Approach a Buyer

### Preparation

Know who you are dealing with. Develop profiles on the president, the senior officers, and the company. There are many possible people to approach in a company, but always start as high in the organization as possible—the president or CEO. He or she might eventually pass you along to someone else, but to these people you will now have more credibility and legitimacy.

Know where they went to school, in what field of study they got a degree, how long they have been in the current position, and a list of previous jobs. You can find this data online at the company website, by searching the Dun & Bradstreet databases, or request a bio about the senior leaders from the company.

The field of degree is important because this might tell you about specific points of view and interests. If an officer's degree is finance, he or she might be interested almost exclusively in the bottom line: profit, higher gross margin, and lower cost of operation. If the background is in marketing and sales, the main concern will probably be new sales, new markets, and greater market share. If a degree is in engineering or science, the officer will still be interested in the bottom line, but might be more interested in technology.

How long the president or other senior officers have been there might indicate how entrepreneurial and aggressive the company is. If someone has been there for thirty years, beware of the NIHS, unless the company has a history otherwise.

Companies that employ the same leaders for over thirty years probably are not too open to ideas from the outside. On the other hand, if the president/CEO has been in the position only a few months, he or she will have a million things on their mind and probably not be able to focus on your ideas. The best leaders to deal with are those who have been there at least a year and were hired with a mandate from the board to aggressively grow the business.

You also want to know what products the company makes, because it will tell you what the core business is and how the company markets. Marketing anything to grow sales or gross margins in products will be a first priority. You also want to know whether the company is in an acquisition mode; the annual report or product literature might tell you that.

You can obtain information on patent assignments to the company by searching Westlaw, an online legal research service, and other databases found online services or at some local libraries. Check the date of assignment and the location of the inventor. This will tell you how many patents the company has, when it got the patents, and whether the patents were generated in-house or purchased from the inventor.

Finally, it is my experience that most large companies see people in one of four categories: vendor, customer, employee, or competition. They don't see people as partners, and they might not see you as one either. If you act like a vendor, with hat in hand, they will treat you like one. And because you don't want to be an employee or a competitor, act like a customer. As described in Chapter 5, be prepared to take purchase orders to the company, if you can.

## First Contact

Find someone who knows the president of the company you want to contact. It is hard to make a "cold call," so network and be imaginative.

Ask your attorney, banker, or accountant if they know anyone with the company. One advantage of a large international law firm, bank, or accounting firm is that they might have this company as a client and can introduce you.

If the company is not a client of your law firm, for example, the company might have in-house attorneys and accountants who your law firm or accountants know. This networking is indirect, but if your accountants can introduce you to their colleagues in a second firm, then that other firm can introduce you to your target buyer company. (Note: This is also a way of getting some extra bang for your legal buck because it costs your attorney nothing to assist you with introductions. They should be glad to do it gratis, because it increases your chance of success and, therefore, their chance of keeping you as a paying client.) The party who ultimately calls the president of the target company to introduce you is probably going to advise him to expect a call from a client of a colleague (you), then will leave your name . . . but this is much better than a cold call.

Other points of contact include a major stockholder, a major customer, a board member, or a college professor of the president or a friend or relative. See if you can get your attorney to introduce you to any one of these people, but you will have to do the work to find the names.

Make a list of key contacts and ask your attorney or accountants if they know any of these people. You might also try your local congressperson. I have asked my congressperson for an appointment to meet in person (it is important to meet in person) at the office to explain my project in that district and to ask for a favor—assistance in introducing me to the congressperson in the district where the company is located.

I then asked the second congressperson to call the company president to set up an appointment. (Note: This strategy only works if your congressperson can see the benefit to the district or to key contributors in the district, and it works only if the second congressperson is interested enough to call the president. The second congressperson won't make a cold call either, so that means that the president must be a politically active person of the same party who knows his congressperson. You have your homework cut out for you, but it will pay off.)

After a second party has paved the way for your call, phone the president of the company and ask for a meeting. Say that you have developed a detailed plan around a new technology for a new market or a way to increase market share estimated to be worth X dollars in the industry.

Don't say that you have an invention to sell. If you do, the president will immediately refer you to someone else, because technology might not be the president's primary interest. It is not even necessary to reveal that you are the inventor at this point; the word "inventor" might carry a certain negative image to a corporate president unless he or she is an engineer or scientist. Do, however, make it clear that you are the owner of the technology, not a broker.

If you can't get through to the president, leave a brief message that you are calling at the suggestion of your mutual acquaintance to set up a meeting to discuss a marketing plan you have developed for this industry. If the first call is not returned in one or two days, call again. If you are unable to get through the second time, ask for voicemail and leave a message regarding your mutual acquaintance, the plan, and the purpose of the proposed meeting. Most corporate presidents have good assistants, but they don't always have the time to take a detailed message, so a voicemail is usually much better. If there is no voicemail, send a fax describing the purpose of the meeting.

Never let your initial contact be by mail or email. It lacks the power of immediacy, might get lost, or is often ignored.

You should be able to explain to the president in less than thirty seconds *what* your technology does and what advantage that might be to the company. Anything more than thirty seconds might lose him or her. Do not waste time explaining *how* it does and what it does. It is none of the president's business at that point. Instead, emphasize the bottom line—profit, new sales, bigger market share, breakthroughs, company image, and other benefits.

Try not to let the president refer you to a vice president (VP) of R&D or, worse, the corporate attorney. The VP of R&D will usually not have the ability to understand and present to management the sales and bottom-line potential of your technology.

Being referred to corporate attorneys is the kiss of death. They have no interest in anything but protecting their backsides; they have "thirty things on their desks" and no interest in technology or increasing sales. They are not visionaries: that's why they don't run companies.

If the president refers you to another corporate officer for the first meeting, indicate that you really prefer to meet the president initially. While you have him or her on the phone, persist in emphasizing the profitability, sales, and marketing projections and the need to explain the broad picture in person.

Say that you think it is important for you to meet in person to get a feel for the company's interest in your plan before you invest more time. Reemphasize that you believe this plan outlines the development of a technology that will increase the bottom line of the company (grow its existing market, reduce costs of operation, create new markets, or whatever the case).

On the phone, if the president persists in referring you to someone else, suggest a meeting with the VP of new business, or marketing and Sales, or R&D (in that order of preference.) Try to get them all in the initial meeting. So long as it is not with the corporate attorney, agree to discuss the plan by phone with the person to whom you are referred and call that person directly, mentioning the president's interest and desire that you meet each other. If you cannot reach the person, leave a message. Meanwhile, contact another company while you are waiting for the return call. If the call isn't returned within a week, take the initiative and call the person to whom you were referred.

## Nondisclosure Agreement

If the president or other officer agrees to a meeting, say that you will first have your attorney send a nondisclosure agreement (see Appendix) for signature. Normally, a nondisclosure agreement is not a problem, but some companies are squeamish because they are concerned that you might reveal something related to a project they are already working on, and by the terms of the nondisclosure agreement you might limit them from developing something that already belongs to them.

It is important to work with your attorney on the precise area of material to be revealed to be sure that you are protected, and that the buyers are comfortable enough to sign it. Remember that the buyers too might be developing products in the area of your invention and will want to know what limits your nondisclosure agreement places on them.

Another reason that it is important to have a signed nondisclosure agreement, drafted by your attorney, in hand before a meeting is that it subtly lets the buyers know that you are more sophisticated than many inventors who don't use attorneys and nondisclosure agreements. They will then know they cannot take advantage of you and they will need to make a legitimate proposal on the purchase.

I have worked with several inventors who refuse to use intellectual property attorneys. In one case, the inventor had a new polymer invention that he thought would make a great coating for roofs. He had tested it extensively. He had several major hotels using it in demonstrations. He did not consult an attorney nor ask the buyer for a nondisclosure agreement because he mistakenly thought that his issued patent would provide enough protection. He met with a prospective buyer in the business of polymer coatings and explained his idea. The buyer was interested, but after several visits for preliminary negotiations, the buyer informed him that they were no longer interested.

In less than a year, the inventor learned that the buyer had started marketing a polymer product for roofing. The inventor was furious. He called me to ask my advice, complaining that he'd been ripped off and his patent was being infringed. So, I contacted the company to inquire about their new product.

The person I spoke with explained that the product was not really new, but the application was. The company was merely selling one of their old products in a new application. It was not infringing upon the inventor's patent. True, the idea for this new application was from the inventor, but because he did not get the advice of an attorney, he proceeded to reveal his marketing plans for his invention without protecting the application.

Another inventor approached me regarding an idea he had to convert solid wastes to fuel by reducing the carbon fraction of municipal garbage and wood waste to small carbon granules without much energy consumption, using a process from the mining industry. The product of his "invention" was a process using ash from the combustion of these granules to improve certain properties in cement.

Unfortunately for him, his patent application was rejected by the USPTO three times, and he had already revealed his idea and much about the use of the ash to several companies in the cement industry. Aided by the advice of an attorney, he would have at least had a nondisclosure agreement in place that might have forced the cement companies to negotiate with him over the rights to use the idea to avoid the threat of his suing them for using his confidential information.

I suggested that he also consider a practical business solution—contact the manufacturer of the process used in the mining industry and offer to acquire an option on the rights to the process for applications outside the mining industry. This could be done for a few thousand dollars.

I suggested he then negotiate with the small independent power producers, who need low-cost fuel, to buy from him the rights to use the carbon-reducing process and agree to sell to him the ash produced by the process, and separately negotiate with the cement industry to buy the ash as a component of its product. Actually, in this case, the inventor declined to pursue this himself, so I offered to do it for him as a partner.

Even with a nondisclosure agreement, it is not necessary or wise to reveal anything more than what the buyer asks. Before the deal is done, it is important to disclose all "material information" to the buyer, because you could be guilty of fraud if some significant information is withheld. Again, a good intellectual property attorney will help ensure that this is not a problem.

# Chapter Nine

## How to Handle Negotiations

This chapter is devoted to suggestions I have found that greatly improve the likelihood of closing a successful deal. They are roughly in the order of their importance, but they are all important.

### Negotiate from a Position of Strength:
### Obtain Multiple Potential Buyers

If buyers know they are the only one you are talking to, they might also come to believe they are the only option you have to sell your technology. Therefore, they will think they can name their price.

To avoid being in this vulnerable position, seek several buyers simultaneously, but do not volunteer that fact to them. In some cases, this upsets the buyer who think you are trying to pressure him or her.

In Japan, I have found they strongly dislike being told that you are talking to other companies. The president of one Japanese company explained this to me like this. It's like telling a girl whom you want to be your girlfriend that you are dating around. She doesn't necessarily mind that you are dating, but she doesn't want to hear about it. However, in the US, most companies do not get too upset to learn you are talking to other prospective buyers. Most expect it.

If the buyer asks for the name of the companies with whom you are talking, you can reply that you are talking to several companies but do not be specific about whom. If the buyer persists, just say that the names of the other companies are confidential. It is less than discreet for you to say others you are negotiating with. This buyer probably would not want you to tell the other companies that you are talking to him or her. Most people will respect your discretion.

If you can manage the timing, get offers from several companies at once. This allows you to have several offers on the table at the same time so you can compare them. It also prevents you from being in the position of having only one option.

### Convince the Buyers That Your Technology Is Real: Host a Demonstration

After the initial meeting at the company site with the president, invite the potential buyer to meet at your location to see a demonstration of the invention. It is important to be credible, and there is nothing better than to see the invention perform.

If your invention is small and can be transported, the visit to your site is not as important. But a visit to your site can also be a measure of interest. If the president comes, the company is interested. If the VP of R&D or another vice president comes, the company might be mildly interested. If the company sends its senior technical person under the VP of R&D, start looking for another buyer.

### Develop a Strategy for the Negotiations

Develop a strategy with your attorney—points to emphasize, how to address hot points (keywords to use), terms you are asking for, and a rationale for why it is reasonable for the buyer to pay for what you are offering.

### Get Help from a Qualified Negotiator

Usually, this person is a business consultant or sophisticated investor in your technology. It should be someone experienced in business negotiations. It might even be your patent attorney or intellectual property attorney.

This tactic lets the buyer know that you are sophisticated enough to use good advisors and that you are not an individual who can easily be taken advantage of. It also gives your associate a chance to meet the buyer and form an opinion regarding the interest and how to proceed in negotiations.

Having your attorney present at the first meeting reduces misunderstandings. Words have different meanings to different people, especially common words that also have legal meanings. Having your attorney at the first meeting should eliminate such misunderstandings ,because the attorney will correct any misuse of legal terms and serve as a listener to help spot when the two parties are not "on the same wavelength." It also allows the attorney to hear the various positions, so he or she can advise you about a revised strategy or different approach.

I am aware of one meeting where the inventor presented his own case and left thinking a deal had been struck. The buyer had not declined the written proposal made by the inventor, who asked for two million dollars and a royalty, and in fact the buyer did say, "We will respond positively; we think we can make a deal."

The inventor flew home first class and celebrated with champagne and a chocolate fudge sundae. The following week, the buyer "responded positively" by sending a completely different contract and set of terms for a proposal. The inventor was shocked. He had read too much into the buyer's statement and did not ask the right questions to determine if the company was indeed accepting *his* proposal. He became disappointed and broke off the negotiations.

Having your attorney at the first meeting or any meeting will offend some buyers. It is completely inappropriate in Japan, for instance. They see negotiations as something that reasonably trustworthy people do together in developing a relationship, and attorneys are present only when there is some major disagreement. They think it is certainly no way to start a relationship based on mutual trust. In a few cases, I have agreed to be present at a first meeting in lieu of the inventor's attorney to avoid offending anyone and to help clarify any misunderstandings.

## Learn Negotiating Skills

Buy yourself a good book on the subject. I recommend *Getting to Yes: Negotiating Agreement without Giving In* by Roger Fisher, William Ury, and Bruce Patton. This is an excellent book resulting from the Harvard Negotiation Project.

I should say at this point that attorneys are not necessarily good negotiators. They know the law. That does not mean they can negotiate. Experience in many negotiations helps to develop negotiating skills, but negotiating is as much art as skill. Besides, your attorney might be a slow learner.

It is fair to ask him or her to assess their negotiating skills and to describe any formal negotiation training they have had since law school. I don't mean to imply that all attorneys are bad negotiators (in fact, they are usually much better than inventors), but they are not always as skilled as a professional negotiator.

## Keep the Discussions Focused

Do not discuss in negotiating sessions any other technologies you own unless your attorney advises you to disclose them to avoid misrepresentation. Resist the temptation to discuss the subject technology in detail. All the buyer needs to know during negotiations is documented in the patent and in any performance data from prototypes that your attorney thinks are appropriate to reveal.

## Avoid All Disagreements if Possible

Differences of opinion related to value are legitimate and occur in every negotiation. However, avoid getting into arguments. Use your attorney to head off or address major disagreements. Let the attorney be the "bad cop" who can work directly with the buyer's attorney when things get nasty. Stay above the fray and cooperate fully with management throughout the negotiations.

## Avoid Indicating a Price

Remember, once you indicate a price, you are stuck with it. You can go lower, but few buyers can ever justify allowing you to raise the price once it tumbles out of your mouth. Don't start the negotiations with estimates of value, which you can't retreat from. In fact, it is usually better to have the buyer mention a value first, from which you can negotiate upward. As a friend of mine says, "He who mentions a dollar figure first—loses!"

If you are maneuvered into stating your price first, it is fine to say that you have made a range of estimates of the value and that you look forward to confirming those numbers with the management. Having said that, I do believe you can save yourself considerable time and disappointment by suggesting that, for example, your estimates lead you to believe the sales might be in a certain range or order of magnitude (such as "ten figures" for sales in the billions) and your selling price is therefore anticipated to be based on that sales volume.

If you give a range of values, make sure that the bottom of the range is the top of what you want. If you say "mid-to-high-seven figures" the buyer will tend to hear the "mid-seven figure" and start to negotiate downward from there.

Personally, I hate to haggle. I enjoy the process of working with the buyer to conclude a deal that will make us both money, but I really hate to bicker over price. I have always enjoyed my Japanese negotiations for that reason. The Japanese always try hard, including opening their valuation process to me for review to come up with a first offer that is the last offer. They hate haggling as much as I do. They know what I would accept before we start and try to accommodate that in their first offer.

The downside to this approach is that there is no room to maneuver. The Japanese could not justify a price that was much higher than the one they initially offered, and they often broke off negotiations if their offer was refused simply because they thought that this indicated negotiations were going nowhere.

There are, of course, people who love to "nickel and dime." It seems to be cultural. They expect you to start high in price and then come down. If they have cut your price in half, they are satisfied. If you insist that there is no room to come down, they might refuse the deal even if it is a good price for them just because they think they will lose face. When you are negotiating with people who love to haggle, double your RTV. If you like these kinds of negotiations, fine; if you don't, then let your attorney do it for you.

## Show Them How Reasonable Your Estimate of Value Is

In Chapter Five, I suggested that you confirm your assumptions about the buyer's market by asking questions at meetings, face to face, then re-estimating the value of your invention, if necessary. When you are ready to talk about terms, walk through each step of your calculations and assumptions so that the buyer can correct any false assumptions, and then conclude with the total amount you are seeking.

This shows you know what you are doing, that you are being reasonable, and that the numbers are not arbitrary. This approach is not only logical, but you are also "leading the witness." Once the buyer has agreed with the assumptions, it is hard to argue with the results.

Consider doing the calculations on a laptop spreadsheet in a meeting with your attorney present. He or she can judge the reaction of the buyer's group and give you good feedback about the next step. When you're negotiating outside the meeting setting, and issues arise that are hard to reconcile, pick up the phone or better yet, go visit the buyer.

Be enthusiastic about working with the buyer (if you are not, maybe you shouldn't be doing it). See yourself as a partner in an ongoing venture. Offer to assist in development of your invention (limited gratis time will be spelled out in the agreement anyway; for additional time you are asked to spend, you should be paid as a consultant). You will be valuable to the company, and it expects you to be a part of the team.

### How to Know When Negotiations Are "Going South"

(These are all actual cases from my own experience.)

- When they agree to a $50,000 "good faith payment" and then send you a check for $25,000.

- When they say they will conclude negotiations in a few weeks, and it takes months (they can't make a decision, or the project has low priority).

- When the president gets fired in the middle of the negotiations (anything you negotiated with him or her just went out the window).

- When the president is not involved or interested in the negotiations at all.

- When the president describes himself as "one good-looking young man" (you're dealing with an oddball).

- When the corporate counsel makes statements like. "I know this will insult you, but . . ."

- When the whole company comes to a stop because its plant in Belgium burned down.

- When you have sent seventy-three faxes during the course of the negotiations, and the company has responded to only four in writing.

- When the key negotiator is fired or dies.

- When a hostile take-over starts.

- When their corporate counsel has your draft agreement for three months before he announces he hasn't read it.

- When they have agreed, weeks ago, in writing on certain key terms, then come back at the last minute to change those terms.

These are all real-life events that have happened to me.

# Chapter Ten

## Dos and Don'ts: The Difference between Failure and Success

The following list is a summary of the main points I've raised in this book. If you follow them, your chances of success are greatly increased.

- Do hire an attorney with specific expertise in specializing in intellectual property.

- Do arrange an introduction to the prospective buyer.

- Do prepare a thorough technical, marketing, and financial analysis prior to contacting potential buyers.

- Do your homework on buyers before you contact them.

- Do your homework on the value of your invention before you discuss number terms.

- Do make sure you have reduced the buyer's risk as much as you can.

- Do be reasonable and understanding of the buyer's position.

- Do be realistic about the value. Don't be grandiose and overestimate the value.

- Do get more than one potential buyer.

- Don't lost faith; be persistent and creative.

- Don't talk to anyone without a signed nondisclosure agreement.

- Don't try to manufacture it yourself. Your time is better spent inventing.

# Chapter Eleven

## How to Determine Your Chances of Success

One thing to consider at this point is what your odds of success might be. Over the years, I have developed a checklist that I use to rate projects.

Write "yes" or "no" to each question. The more yes answers, the lower the risk to you and possible investors. If you have more yes than no responses, then you have a better than fifty-fifty chance of succeeding.

The shaded boxes are critical, and a "no" in any of these could be fatal. If you answer no in both of the two shaded boxes in either pair, you are likely not going to succeed.

For example, if you don't have any chance of protecting your technology, then you don't really have anything to sell. If you don't really have the experience necessary to run a company based on your technology, and you aren't willing to consider leaving the operations to others who do, you probably will never get adequate financing.

Ask yourself these questions and be brutally honest. If you answer yes to all, then you have a good chance of success. Each no answer means you are less likely to succeed.

### Checklist for Project Viability

| Question | Yes | No |
|---|---|---|
| Do I have anything unique? | | |
| Do I have any patentable/copyrighted material? | | |
| Am I free of other inventors with possible claims? | | |
| Am I free of possible employer claims on technology? | | |
| Have I applied for a patent? | | |
| Were my USPTO actions positive? | | |
| Do I have a patent issued? | | |
| Is all the gateway technology fully tested and demonstrated at lab/bench scale? | | |
| Is the technology past the research stage? | | |
| Is the prototype tested successfully? | | |
| Do I make a credible presentation to top managers? | | |
| Do I have a national reputation in the industry? | | |
| Am I capable of running a company? | | |
| Am I willing to have someone else run the company? | | |
| Can I get along with potential partners? | | |
| Am I financially solvent to survive until financing? | | |
| Can I focus? | | |
| Do I have a professionally reviewed financing plan? | | |
| Do I have legal counsel respected by venture investors? | | |
| Is my first product identified? | | |
| Do I have a second product? | | |
| Is my first market defined? | | |
| Is the annual market for my technology at least $100 million? | | |
| Is my market free of significant competition? | | |
| Is my cost of goods less than 30 percent? | | |
| Is my annual profit at least $1 million? | | |
| Would a VC invest in this project? | | |
| Would I invest in this project? | | |
| **Totals** | | |

# Appendix

The following appendix includes sample agreements. Please note: These are samples. You should use them only on the advice of a qualified attorney. They are intended as a basis for review of the issues, and allocations of risks, which are specific to each case.

However, these agreements should save you some money on legal fees because you are not starting from scratch. The issues unique to your case are what your attorney will focus on, along with the specific laws in the state where you reside and any recent changes in law.

# Sample Assignment Agreement

These are actual agreements I have used.
You should DEFINITELY consult your attorney for
additional terms that might be critical to your specific situation.

This Agreement is effective this _____ day of ___*(effective date)*_____, 20__, by and between _____*(your name)*_____ , hereinafter called LICENSOR, having his/her principal address at _____*(your address)*_____, and XYZ Corporation, a _____*(name of state)*_____ corporation, hereinafter called LICENSEE, having its principal address at _____*(LICENSEE'S ADDRESS)*_____.

RECITALS

A.      LICENSOR owns all rights, title, and interest in and to the "TECHNOLOGY" described on Exhibit A attached hereto.

B.      LICENSEE desires to purchase from LICENSOR full right and title to the TECHNOLOGY.

NOW,            THEREFORE, for and in consideration of the mutual covenants herein, LICENSOR and LICENSEE agree as follows:

AGREEMENT

1.      Assignment.    LICENSEE assigns all right, title and interest in and to the TECHNOLOGY, including all patents, trade secrets, and other intellectual property, on a worldwide basis.

*(Section 1 is the key operative provision of the agreement. It assigns all right, title, and interest to the TECHNOLOGY on a worldwide basis to XYZ. Technology is defined in the recital by reference to Exhibit A)*

2.      Consideration.

*("Consideration" is the bargained for exchange of rights and benefits. The assignor (LICENSOR) provides TECHNOLOGY in exchange for money)*

(a)     Up-Front Payment. LICENSEE will pay to LICENSOR $_____ within five days of signing this Agreement. This payment is nonrefundable and will not be credited against the royalty due under subsection (b).

*(The agreement states the up-front payment is nonrefundable to protect the assignor)*

(b)     Royalty on Sales. LICENSEE will pay to LICENSOR, within 10 days of the end of each calendar quarter, ____% on the gross income from the sale, lease, sub-license, assignment or other transfer of any products using or incorporating the TECHNOLOGY or the TECHNOLOGY itself by LICENSEE during such quarter. With each royalty payment above LICENSEE agrees to provide to LICENSOR a written report listing the calculation made to determine the royalties owed and paid. LICENSEE further agrees to keep records sufficient to verify and support the reports specified herein.

*(The base for calculating the royalty percentage is gross income. In some transactions, net income or net receipts or other base is used for royalty calculations. Royalty payments are paid quarterly (as opposed to every 6 months or annually) which is helpful to the assignor of the TECHNOLOGY since payments streams will come more quickly. In some cases, 10 days after the end of the calendar quarter may not be enough time for royalties to be calculated.*

*The license fee of Subsection 2(a), a one-time up-front payment, has no credit value against the ongoing "running" royalty of Subsection 2(b). In some cases, the up-front payment is a credit in whole or part toward the running royalty. The assignee may also negotiate for a "cap" or limit on running royalty payments.)*

LICENSEE warrants that it will take no actions to manipulate the royalties or calculation of royalties it gets for the purpose of reducing royalty payments to LICENSOR.

(c)     Taxes. Payments by LICENSEE hereunder do not include sales, use, excise, withholding and any other taxes or duties due ay any taxing authority in connection with this Agreement. LICENSEE will pay all such taxes (except for any taxes on LICENSOR' net income), if any, to the appropriate taxing authorities.

(d)     <u>Reports and Audit</u>. With each payment due from LICENSEE under sections 3(b), and (c) above, LICENSEE will provide LICENSOR with a written report in which the calculations used to determine such payments are described. Furthermore, in order to verify the amounts payable by LICENSEE hereunder, LICENSEE agrees to permit LICENSOR to audit all relevant records of LICENSEE, upon reasonable notice and during regular business hours. Such audits will be at LICENSOR' expense, but will be at LICENSEE'S expense if such audit shows that LICENSEE has underpaid LICENSOR by 5% or more.

*(This contains the right for LICENSOR to audit relevant records of XYZ. The owner of TECHNOLOGY needs leverage to make sure that royalty payments are calculated and paid properly and timely. The number of audits is usually limited for a specific period, for example, one per year. The last sentence is intended to be an incentive for proper calculations, since if the royalty exceeds a certain amount, 5% in this case, the assignee must pay for the cost of the audit.)*

(e)     <u>Payment terms.</u> All payments will be made in United States dollars, free of any currency control or other restrictions to LICENSOR at the address designated by LICENSOR. Unless otherwise agreed by LICENSOR in writing, LICENSEE will pay all amounts due by certified check or wire transfer to a bank account designated by LICENSOR.

(f)     <u>Interest.</u> Interest will accrue on any delinquent amounts owed by LICENSEE under Section 2 at the lesser of eighteen percent (18%) per annum or the maximum rate permitted by applicable usury law.

*(This is a deterrent and hammer to motivate the assignee to make payment on time.)*

(g)     <u>No Setoff.</u> LICENSEE will not setoff or offset against amounts owed to the LICENSOR that LICENSEE claims are due to it. LICENSEE agrees to bring any claims or causes of action it may have in a separate action and waives any right it may have to offset, setoff, or withhold payments owed to the LICENSOR.

*(The no setoff provision is intended to have payments be as invulnerable as possible against any other claims relating to the TECHNOLOGY.)*

(h)    Fee for Identified Project Sales. (This is relevant only if you intend to assist the assignee with sales.) In return for identifying in writing for LICENSEE and/or its dealers, and assisting in the closing of projects to which LICENSEE and/or its dealers may sell products using or incorporating the TECHNOLOGY, LICENSEE will pay a fee to LICENSOR equal to:

(1)    _____% of the amounts gotten by LICENSEE or its dealers from any such project on the sale, lease, or other transfer of products using or incorporating the TECHNOLOGY (payable within 15 days of LICENSEE'S receipt of such amounts); and

(2)    40% of the marginal increase of royalty income actually gotten by LICENSEE from any such project from the use of equipment and supplies utilizing the TECHNOLOGY (payable within 10 days of the end of each calendar quarter).

An initial list of such projects identified by LICENSOR is set forth on Exhibit B hereto. LICENSOR may add to the projects on this list at any time.

4.    LICENSOR Warranties.

LICENSOR represents and warrants to LICENSEE that LICENSOR is the sole and exclusive owner of the TECHNOLOGY and the rights assigned in this Agreement to LICENSEE; that LICENSOR has not previously assigned and will not attempt to grant any rights in this TECHNOLOGY or any derivative work or improvement based on the TECHNOLOGY to any third party; that LICENSOR has full power to enter into this Agreement and to assign all right, title, and interest in and to the technology to LICENSEE.

*(The assignor is representing and warranting that he has ownership to the TECHNOLOGY. This is very important representation and warranty to the assignee and one that may be a deal breaker if not given. In this case, the assignee would request these presentations and warranties be on a worldwide basis to match the scope of the assignment. The assignor should not give this warranty without making sure that he, in fact, does own the TECHNOLOGY. One of the key areas of*

*vulnerability is patents that may be embodied in the TECHNOLOGY since it is difficult or impossible to ever know what patents might be applicable to TECHNOLOGY. The assignor may try to qualify his level of assurance to the "best of my knowledge.")*

5.      LICENSEE'S Representations.

LICENSEE represents and warrants to LICENSOR that LICENSEE has the full power to enter into this Agreement and to carry out its obligations under this Agreement.

*(This is a very simple representation from the assignee that it has the power to enter into the agreement and to carry out its obligations. This is a good paper warranty, but an assignor should conduct due diligence to make sure the assignee has the financial resources to make the payments that will be required under the agreement.)*

6.      Delivery and Acceptance of the TECHNOLOGY.

The parties acknowledge and agree that, upon exercise of the Option hereunder, LICENSOR will have delivered to LICENSEE in full the TECHNOLOGY. Further, upon such exercise, LICENSEE will have used and accepted the TECHNOLOGY in full, with no further obligations to install or support such for LICENSEE (unless under the terms of a separate support agreement).

*(The exhibit is intended to define what tangible items must be delivered. TECHNOLOGY is often delivered both by tangible media as well as through technical assistance. The assignor should try to avoid acceptance and simply give the representation and warranty since an acceptance procedure can be used by the assignee to delay payment.)*

7.      Technology Support.

Upon exercise of the Option, LICENSEE may either: (a) have LICENSOR maintain and upgrade the TECHNOLOGY on a mutually agreed fixed price bid basis on an hourly basis; or (b) maintain and enhance the TECHNOLOGY by any other means or manner of payment.

*(Since it is the assignor's TECHNOLOGY, there may be a continuing obligation to provide technical assistance to assure that XYZ can practically exploit the TECHNOLOGY. In this provision, the assignee has the obligation to upgrade the TECHNOLOGY on a fixed price bid basis or an hourly basis. The assignor must define its support obligations very carefully to be certain it understands what it must do. For example, what does upgrade and enhance mean? If not defined by the assignor, the scope of the obligations may not be commensurate with the payments received.)*

8.      Protection of Proprietary Rights.

LICENSOR and LICENSEE acknowledge that the TECHNOLOGY is of a character which is or may be protectable by patent, trade secrecy, and/or copyright under the laws of the United States and other countries. LICENSOR agrees to cooperate with LICENSEE in obtaining patent, trademark, copyright, and other statutory protections for the TECHNOLOGY at LICENSEE'S expense, and LICENSOR hereby authorizes LICENSEE to execute in LICENSEE'S name an application for patent or copyright registration of the TECHNOLOGY and such other documents of registration and recordation as may be necessary to perfect in LICENSEE the rights assigned LICENSEE hereunder in each country in which the TECHNOLOGY is sold, distributed, or sublicensed. All proprietary rights in any portion of any derivative work or improvement based on the TECHNOLOGY will be owned exclusively by LICENSEE. LICENSOR hereby authorizes LICENSEE to use the trademarks and trade names of LICENSEE'S choosing in marketing the TECHNOLOGY.

*(LICENSOR, as the inventor, agrees to cooperate with the assignee in order to obtain intellectual property protection for the TECHNOLOGY. Cooperation would usually include the obligation for LICENSOR to sign any registration applications if the author or inventor's signature is needed.*

*With respect to the last two sentences, normally the assignee will own all right, title, and interest in and to any improvements or derivative works based on the TECHNOLOGY. Further, if it is XYZ's TECHNOLOGY, LICENSOR typically would not authorize XYZ to use the trademarks and trade names with respect to marketing the TECHNOLOGY, unless LICENSOR has already used such trademarks and those are part of the assignment. The assignment language would normally assign all right, title, and interest and all intellectual property rights relating to or connected to the TECHNOLOGY, including trademarks.)*

9.      Nondisclosure.

LICENSEE and LICENSOR agree that the terms and conditions of this Agreement, the concepts, know-how and techniques known or developed by LICENSOR at the time of entering into this Agreement and embodies in the TECHNOLOGY, any other information concerning either party's marketing plans, existing or future products OR other confidential business or technical information disclosed in the furtherance of this Agreement will be deemed confidential to the disclosing party and held in strict confidence and will not be disclosed or used without the express written consent of the disclosing party. Notwithstanding the above, the following materials will not be deemed confidential:

(a)     Information which at the time of disclosure is in the public domain;

(b)     Information which after disclosure is published or otherwise becomes part of the public domain through no fault of either party (but only after, and only to the extent that, it is published or otherwise becomes a part of the public domain;

(c)     Information which can be shown was gotten from a third party who did not acquire it, directly or indirectly, under an obligation of confidence,

the TECHNOLOGY and LICENSOR would be obligated to keep it secret.)

*(Since the assignee (XYZ) is the owner, XYZ would not have a nondisclosure obligation during the period of the agreement except until all payments are made. In the payment provision (Section (2), there is often a cap on the total payments at which time at which a nondisclosure obligation on the part of the assignee would terminate.*

*The nondisclosure provision, as it applies to XYZ, must prohibit XYZ from marketing and distributing products such as mass marketed products.*

*LICENSOR, as the assignor, no longer owns the TECHNOLOGY and LICENSOR would be obligated to keep it a secret.)*

## 10.     Trademarks.

Any trademarks used by LICENSOR to identify the TECHNOLOGY, except for LICENSOR' name, are hereby assigned by LICENSOR to LICENSEE. Any trademarks adopted and used by LICENSEE in the marketing of the TECHNOLOGY will be the sole property of LICENSEE. LICENSEE will have the sole responsibility for ensuring that any such trademarks do not infringe the rights of third parties.

*(This is the trademark assignment for the TECHNOLOGY.)*

11.  <u>Reversion of Ownership for Nonpayment.</u> *This is extremely unusual.*

LICENSEE understands and agrees that if it fails to make payment to LICENSOR within 10 days of LICENSOR' written notice of any overdue payment, then LICENSOR may elect to have all ownership rights to the TECHNOLOGY revert from LICENSEE— and deny LICENSEE any interest or rights in such from the date of LICENSOR' assumption. LICENSEE agrees to cooperate to sign any additional documents requested by LICENSOR in order to perfect such reassignment. Ownership of the TECHNOLOGY will also revert to LICENSOR in the event that LICENSEE files for bankruptcy or otherwise ceases to conduct business. [NOTE THAT THIS SECTION IS SUBJECT TO REVISION PENDING REVIEW BY TAX COUNSEL REGARDING CAPITAL GAINS TREATMENT.]

*(This attempts to have ownership revert back to LICENSOR in the event of nonpayment. A full assignment back is needed. This is an unusual remedy. The last sentence of the paragraph dealing with bankruptcy is not enforceable under U.S. Bankruptcy Law.)*

12.  <u>Consequential Damages.</u>

Under no other circumstances will either party to this Agreement be liable to the other party for indirect, special, incidental, or consequential damages or the loss of anticipated profits arising from any breach of this Agreement by the other party even if notice is given of the possibility of such damages.

*(This is a fairly standard disclaimer of consequential damages. The "laundry list" of types of damages excluded would be special, indirect, incidental, consequential damages. The reason for a longer list is that judges characterize these damages differently so that the longer list tries to cover all characterizations of types of damages that would be excluded. The specific mention of the loss of anticipated profits is helpful because sometimes profits are not included within consequential damages.*

*The general principal of law is that you are not liable for consequential damages unless you are aware of the possibility of such damages. The last phase "even if notice is given of the possibility of such damages" is intended to exclude such damages in the case where a party could be liable for consequential damages because notice of possibility was given.*

*The assignor must carefully consider whether consequential damages should be excluded since it is his TECHNOLOGY. Having the assignee be responsible for consequential damages can be good leverage and a deterrent to breaches of the agreement.)*

13.    <u>General Terms.</u>

(a)    <u>Entire Agreement</u>. This Agreement and the Exhibits attached hereto constitute the entire agreement between the parties relating to the assignment. No amendment or modification of this agreement may be made except by an instrument in writing signed by both parties.

*(The entire agreement clause is intended to make sure that the written agreement, not verbal agreements, cover the agreement between the parties.)*

(b)    <u>No Assignment</u>. Except for an acquisition or purchase of substantially all of the assets of LICENSEE, this Agreement may not be assigned in whole or in party by LICENSEE without the prior written consent of LICENSOR, which consent will not be unreasonably withheld. LICENSOR may assign LICENSOR' interest in all or part of the payments due LICENSOR hereunder upon notice in writing to LICENSEE.

*(This is a limitation on assignment particularly for the assignee. If payment were all made up-front or following all payments to the assignor, no limitation on the assignee's right to further transfer the TECHNOLOGY could be made. This is drafted such that the assignee could assign but there would be breach of contract but the assignment would not be void. In order to void such an assignment, a clause must be added that any attempted assignment would be void and of no effect.)*

(c)    Governing Law. This Agreement will be governed and interpreted in accordance with the laws of the State of California, excluding that body of law known as conflicts of law. Except as herein otherwise provided, the parties agree that any dispute arising under this Agreement will be resolved in the state or federal courts within the State of California and LICENSEE expressly consents to jurisdiction therein. Venue for any legal action will be the state courts of Sacramento County, California, and the federal courts of the Northern District of California.

*(This addresses governing law. The first sentence indicates the agreement will be governed by the substantive law of the State of California. This is stated as "will be governed by the laws of the State of California excluding that body of law known as conflicts of laws." Each state has conflict of law provisions which, in the absence of a governing law provision, will determine what state law will apply to the agreement. If the agreement merely says "will be governed by the laws of the State of California" then these conflicts of law provisions will be considered to determine what state law will apply.)*

*The next sentence starts with "Except as herein otherwise provided..." It is not clear if there are any exceptions since there is no arbitration provision. This sentence attempts to indicate in what courts the dispute will be handled and that the assignee expressly consents to jurisdiction therein. The assignor wants a form of dispute between the parties. The last sentence indicates the venue, that is specific courts for handling such a dispute.*

*Arbitration may be an appropriate dispute resolution mechanism, at least for payment disputes. The assignor should always reserve the right to go to court to obtain a temporary restraining order and other equitable relief in the cases of intellectual property abuse.)*

(d)　　Notice. Any notice required or permitted to be sent hereunder will be deemed delivered on the date mailed or otherwise dispatched if mailed, postage prepaid, by registered, express or certified mail, return receipt requested, or by nationally-recognized private express courier, to either party at the address listed above, or such other addresses of which either party may so notify the other.

*(This provision needs to be followed carefully if a legal notice must be sent to the other party. If notice is not sent in accordance with the provision, then notice has not been given. Permitting notice by confirmed fax would be consistent with current communication methods.)*

(e)　　Independent Contractor. LICENSOR will be deemed to have the status of an independent contractor to LICENSEE, and nothing in this Agreement will be deemed to place the parties in the relationship of employer-employee, principal-agent, partners, or joint venturers.

*(The purpose of this provision is for each part to attempt to avoid having liability for the other as partners or principal and agent. While it is self-serving, a court will consider it as some evidence of what relationship is intended.)*

(f)　　Attorney's Fees. In the event that any legal action, including arbitration, is required in order to enforce or interpret any of the provisions of this Agreement, the prevailing party in such action will recover all reasonable costs and expenses, including attorney's fees, incurred in connection therewith.

*(Under California law, this must be equally applicable to both parties. A one-sided attorney's fees provision, that is, if the assignor wins the assignor's fees are paid but not the opposite, is not permitted.)*

(g)　　Waiver. The failure of either party to enforce any provision of this Agreement will not be deemed a waiver of that or any other provision of this Agreement.

*(This provision indicates that the failure to take action in one instance will not be a waiver of any rights of that particular provision or any other provision of the agreement. This is intended to keep all remedies intact.)*

(h)　<u>Force Majeure</u>. Neither party will be deemed in default of this Agreement to the extent that performance of their obligations or attempts to cure any breach are delayed or prevented by reason of any act of God, fire, natural disaster, accident, act of government, shortages of material or supplies or any other cause beyond the control of such party, provided that such party gives the other party written notice thereof promptly and, in any event, within 15 days of discovery thereof and uses its good faith efforts to cure the breach. In the event of such a Force Majeure, the time for performance or cure will be extended for a period equal to the duration of the Force Majeure but not in excess of 6 months.

*(This is not always used because it provides an excuse to performance. Here the TECHNOLOGY has already been developed and delivery dates are not of concern. Therefore, it may be to the assignor's disadvantage not to have a Force Majeure provision because it might be used by XYZ as an excuse for payment or for a breach of confidentiality provision.)*

(i)　<u>Headings.</u> The headings of the Sections of this Agreement are for convenience only and will not be of any effect in construing the meanings of the provisions.

IN WITNESS WHEREOF, the parties hereto have executed this agreement as of the date first written above.

XYZ Corporation

By: ____(LICENSEE'S SIGNATURE)_____

Its: _____(SIGNOR'S TITLE)_____

By: ____(LICENSOR'S SIGNATURE)_____

　　　John Z. LICENSOR

# Sample License Agreement

This Agreement is effective this _____ day of ____*(effective date)*_____, 20__, by and between _____*(your name)*_____ , hereinafter called LICENSOR, having his/her principal address at _____*(your address)*_____, and XYZ Corporation, a _____*(name of state)*_____ corporation, hereinafter called LICENSEE, having its principal address at _____*(LICENSEE'S ADDRESS)*_____.

*(The first issue to consider is the definition of the "licensee." It is defined as a single corporation, but sometimes "licensee" is defined very broadly to include a family of corporations rather than a single corporation. The greater the scope of licensees, the more potential revenue is lost and also the greater the vulnerability of the TECHNOLOGY.)*

## RECITALS

WHEREAS, LICENSOR owns all right, title and interest in and to the "TECHNOLOGY" described on Exhibit A attached hereto ("TECHNOLOGY"); and

WHEREAS, LICENSOR and LICENSEE desire that LICENSEE be authorized to manufacture, promote, and sell (NOTE: you may choose to limit rights to either manufacturing or marketing or both) the TECHNOLOGY for a _____ year period under the term and conditions set forth below.

NOW, THEREFORE, for and in consideration of the mutual covenants herein, LICENSOR and LICENSEE agree as follows:

## 1.    License

*(There are many possible operative terms in the license grant. The normal operative words for a patent license are to make, use, and sell. In the case of a copyrighted work, the operative words would be to copy and distribute, and in some cases, to prepare derivative works.*

*If a right is not expressly granted, the licensee does not have it. First, is the license exclusive or nonexclusive? Here, it is exclusive and the territory is worldwide. There is no sublicense right. The activities that may be carried out on a worldwide exclusive basis are to use, incorporate within its products, manufacture, promote and sell the TECHNOLOGY.*

*Normally, TECHNOLOGY is defined to include the proprietary information and know how, and there would not be any separation. Also, Exhibit B is intended to be a field of use limitation to applications for which the TECHNOLOGY could be used on an exclusive basis.*

*Normally, the license to the TECHNOLOGY is the right to make products, with product sales being what royalties are based on.)*

(a) <u>Grant of License</u>. Subject to the terms of this agreement, LICENSOR grants to LICENSEE an exclusive worldwide (again, you may choose to restrict the territory to that geographical area the license best represents) license covered in (b) below to manufacture, use and sell products using or incorporating the TECHNOLOGY, in and limited to the applications set forth in <u>Exhibit B</u> (the "<u>Applications</u>"). This license does not include LICENSEE other applications not listed on Exhibit B and does not include the right to sublicense.

(b) <u>License Restrictions</u>. Notwithstanding Section 1 (a) above, LICENSEE understands and agrees that (i) the license granted to LICENSEE hereunder is limited to the period as provided in Sections 7(a) and 7(c) below, and (ii) LICENSOR reserves all rights with respect to any and all applications not listed on Exhibit B.

*(The one-year term is unusually short since it takes time to get a product into the marketplace. Normally, a license period would be much longer.)*

(c) <u>Transfer of Technology</u>. Promptly following the execution of this Agreement, LICENSOR will provide LICENSEE with a copy of documentation, drawings, memoranda, other written descriptions and models, samples or other physical examples of the TECHNOLOGY which is available and is reasonably needed by LICENSEE to understand and commercially utilize and implement the TECHNOLOGY. LICENSOR will also make available to LICENSEE technicians and scientists employed or retained by LICENSOR familiar with the TECHNOLOGY to assist LICENSEE in the transfer of the TECHNOLOGY accordance with Section 2(d) below.

*(This provision deals with the delivery of the TECHNOLOGY. The last sentence deal with technical assistance which may be needed in order for the licensee to fully use the TECHNOLOGY. TECHNOLOGY is defined in <u>Exhibit A</u>.)*

(d)     Ownership. LINCESOR owns all right, title, and interest in and to TECHNOLOGY and all intellectual property rights and interests incorporated therein. LICENSOR will also own all right, title, and interest in and to any derivative works or improvements made by or for LICENSEE to the TECHNOLOGY.

*(This provision indicates that LICENSOR retains all right, title, and interest and into the TECHNOLOGY. It also states that LICENSOR will own all right, title, and interest in and modifications and enhancements of the TECHNOLOGY. The operative terms in the case of a patent are improvement, and, in the case of copyright, derivative works.)*

(e)     Modifications and/or Enhancements. A modifications or enhancements to the TECHNOLOGY made by or for LICENSEE (including but not limited to those under Section 2(b) below) will require LICENSOR' prior written consent, which consent will not be unreasonably withheld. LICENSEE agrees in all cases to verity to LICENSOR that such activities do not compromise the safety or proprietary nature of the TECHNOLOGY.

*(This is a further restriction, not in the license grant, that LICENSEE must have Jone's written consent before any modifications or enhancements may be made to the TECHNOLOGY.)*

2.     Obligations of LICENSEE.

*(In the case of an exclusive license, the licensee often is allocated quantitative requirements in terms for marketing and distribution of products. The sales or revenue quota must be met in order for the exclusivity to be retained.)*

(a)     Manufacture, Promotion, and Sale of TECHNOLOGY. LICENSEE agrees to use its best efforts to manufacture, promote, and vigorously sell products using or incorporating the TECHNOLOGY in connection with the Applications in order to achieve maximum benefit to the parties hereto.

(b)     Adaptation. LICENSEE agrees to make, at its expense, such changes to TECHNOLOGY as would be appropriate to adapt the TECHNOLOGY for use in the Applications and are required to comply with local and state law, and the law of any countries, in which the TECHNOLOGY is sold and used.

LICENSEE further agrees to consult with LICENSOR as to any changes to the TECHNOLOGY pursuant to this Section 2(b). LICENSEE hereby assigns to LICENSOR all of its right, title, and interest in all such adaptations including but not limited to all related patent, copyright trade secret, and moral rights.

*(This requires LICENSEE to bear the expense of any changes to TECHNOLOGY as needed to adapt TECHNOLOGY for use in the application. However, Sections 2(b) and 1(e) need to be coordinated better because it is not clear how these two fits together.)*

(c) <u>LICENSEE Personnel</u>. LICENSEE agrees to train and maintain a sufficient number of capable technical and marketing personnel having the knowledge and training necessary to: (i) properly inform dealers and other customers concerning the features and capabilities of products using or incorporating the TECHNOLOGY and, if necessary, competitive products; (ii) service and support products using or incorporating the TECHNOLOGY; and (iii) otherwise carry out the obligations and responsibilities of LICENSEE under this Agreement.

*(This requires the licensee to train and maintain capable technical marketing personnel. The intent is to make sure that the licensee exploits that TECHNOLOGY fully in order to generate revenues for the licensor.)*

(d) <u>Mutual Service and Support</u>.

(i) <u>Support Provided by LICENSEE</u>. LICENSEE agrees to provide prompt pre- and post-sales service and support to LICENSOR for sales made by LICENSOR pursuant to Section 3(k) below of all TECHNOLOGY equipment, supplies, and methodologies.

(ii) <u>Support Provided by LICENSOR</u> will be available to provide LICENSEE with reasonable service and support at LICENSEE'S written request during the term of this Agreement. Such support will consist of consulting services in conjunction with the transfer of the TECHNOLOGY. The first ____ hours of such support, including instruction and training, will be provided to LICENSEE free-of-charge, with all support above ____ hours being provided by LICENSOR at $____/hour. All reasonable expenses incurred in providing such support will be reimbursed by LICENSEE.

*(Support and service is extremely important in order for revenue streams to be generated. Licensor must carefully determine the scope of the support obligation it undertakes to make sure it can actually perform and that the payments for such performance are reasonable.)*

(e)    LICENSEE Covenants. LICENSEE agrees to: (i) make no false or misleading representations with regard to LICENSOR or the TECHNOLOGY; and (ii) make no representations, warranties, or guarantees to customers or to the trade with respect to the specifications, features, or capabilities of the TECHNOLOGY that are inconsistent with the specifications listed on Exhibit A.

*(This is another quality control provision to try to make sure the licensee's actions do not create any problems for the licensor.)*

(f)    Compliance with Law. LICENSEE agrees to comply with all applicable international, national, state, regional, and local laws and regulations in performing its duties hereunder and in any of its dealings with respect to the TECHNOLOGY.

*(This is the obligation of the licensee to comply with all applicable laws.)*

(g)    Compliance with U.S. Export Laws. LICENSEE agrees not to export or re-export (directly or indirectly) the TECHNOLOGY or any products using or incorporating the TECHNOLOGY without complying with the U.S. Export Administration Act of 1979, as amended and the regulations thereunder.

*(Sometimes such as U.S. export control law provision is combined with the general compliance with law provision. The actual language that must go into a U.S. export law provisions depends on the TECHNOLOGY and the destinations where it may be exported. In a worldwide license, this provision must reflect the most restrictive countries.)*

(h)    Governmental Approval. If any approval with respect to this Agreement, or the notification or registration thereof, will be required at any time during the term of this Agreement, with respect to giving legal effect to this Agreement in any country, or with respect to compliance with exchange regulations or other requirements so as to assure the right of remittance abroad of U.S. dollars pursuant to this Agreement or otherwise, LICENSEE agrees to immediately take whatever steps may be necessary in this respect, and any charges incurred in connection therewith will be the responsibility of LICENSEE. LICENSEE further agrees to keep LICENSOR currently informed of its efforts in this connection. LICENSOR will be under no obligation hereunder until LICENSEE has provided LICENSOR with satisfactory evidence that such approval, notification, or registration is not required or that it has been obtained.

*(In some cases, particularly in developing countries, governmental approvals are needed for purposes of enforceability and payment. In a few countries, a technology transfer agency must approve any TECHNOLOGY transfer into the country.)*

(i) <u>Market Conditions</u>. LICENSEE agrees to advice LICENSOR promptly concerning any market information that comes to LICENSEE's attention respecting LICENSOR, the TECHNOLOGY, LICENSOR' market position or the continued competitiveness of the TECHNOLOGY in the marketplace. LICENSEE will confer with LICENSOR from time to time at the request of LICENSOR on matters relating to market conditions, sales forecasting, and product planning relating to the TECHNOLOGY.

*(This is an obligation on the part of the licensee to keep the licensor informed as to the market status of the TECHNOLOGY.)*

(j) <u>Costs and Expenses</u>. Except as expressly provided herein or agreed to in writing by LICENSOR and LICENSEE, LICENSEE agrees to pay all costs and expenses incurred in the performance of LICENSEE's obligations under this Agreement.

(k) <u>Inspection</u>. LICENSOR may, upon reasonable notice, enter any premises of LICENSEE to inspect the products, uses and methodologies utilizing or incorporating the TECHNOLOGY.

*(This is a general right of inspection. This can be helpful to make sure the licensee's confidentiality obligations are being followed.)*

3. <u>Compensation.</u>

*(There is no up-front license fee. The royalty base is gross sales price with respect to any products sold that incorporate the TECHNOLOGY. An up-front license payment is a good way to determine the good faith of the licensee with respect to payments.)*

(a)    Royalty on Sales. LICENSEE agrees to pay to LICENSOR, within 10 days of the end of each calendar quarter, a ____% royalty on the gross sales price of sale, lease, or other transfer by LICENSEE of any products using or incorporating the TECHNOLOGY during such quarter. With each payment above, LICENSEE agrees to provide to LICENSOR a written report listing the calculation made to determine the commissions owed and paid. LICENSEE further agrees to keep records sufficient to verify and support the reports specified herein.

LICENSEE warrants that it will take no actions to manipulate the royalties or calculation of royalties it gets for the purpose of reducing royalty payments to LICENSOR.

(b)    Taxes. Payment of commissions and royalties by LICENSEE do not include sales, use, excise, withholding and any other taxes or duties due by any taxing authority in connection with this Agreement. LICENSEE will pay all such taxes (except for any taxes on LICENSOR' net income), if any, to the appropriate taxing authorities.

*(Since there are other international provisions, responsibility for withholding taxes should be allocated. Withholding taxes can be payable even if the licensor does not have any permanent establishment, that is, a direct tax presence in another country. For example, if LICENSEE were a Japanese party, there would be a 10% withholding tax on the license fee and royalties, and the Japanese party would withhold that from the royalty payments to the licensor. There is no economic impact if licensor can fully use the withholding tax as a credit against tax liability. Many individuals or small companies cannot. The licensor's price must be grossed-up in order for the licensor to receive what is expected.)*

(c)    Reports and Audit. With each payment due from LICENSEE under Sections 3(a) and (b) above, LICENSEE will provide LICENSOR with a written report in which the calculations used to determine such payments are described. Furthermore, in order to verify the amounts payable by LICENSEE hereunder, LICENSEE agrees to permit LICENSOR to audit all relevant records of

LICENSEE, upon reasonable notice and during regular business hours. Such audits will be at LICENSOR' expense, but will be at LICENSEE's expense if such audit shows that LICENSEE has underpaid LICENSOR by 5% or more.

(d) <u>Payment Terms</u>. All payments shall be made in United States dollars, free of any currency control or other restrictions to LICENSOR at the address designated by LICENSOR. Unless otherwise agreed by LICENSOR in writing, LICENSEE will pay all amounts due by certified check or wire transfer to a bank account designated by the LICENSOR.

(e) <u>Interest</u>. Interest shall accrue on any delinquent amounts owed by LICENSEE under this Section 3 at the lesser of eighteen percent (18%) per annum or the maximum rate permitted by applicable usury law.

(f) <u>No Setoff</u>. LICENSEE will not setoff or offset against amounts owed to the LICENSOR that LICENSEE claims are due to it. LICENSEE agrees to bring any claims or causes of action it may have in a separate action and waives any right it may have to offset, setoff or withhold payments owed to the LICENSOR.

4. <u>LICENSEE Determines Its Own Price.</u>

LICENSEE will be entirely free to determine the actual prices at which any products using or incorporating the TECHNOLOGY will be sold to its customers.

*(This is intended to make clear there is no resale price maintenance, that is, setting prices in downstream distribution channels. This provision should refer to the products which embody the TECHNOLOGY.)*

5. <u>Patents, Patent Markings, Trademarks, Trade Names, Logos, Designations, and Copyrights.</u>

(a) <u>Use During Agreement</u>. During the term of this Agreement, LICENSEE is authorized to use LICENSOR' patent markings, trademarks, trade names, logos, and designations used by

LICENSOR for the TECHNOLOGY in accordance with LICENSOR reasonable instructions. LICENSEE agrees to identify all products using or incorporating the TECHNOLOGY as manufactured under license from LICENSOR, and to use appropriate patent markings or designations of patent status on the TECHNOLOGY. LICENSEE understands and agrees that it has paid no consideration for the use of LICENSOR' trademarks, trade names, logos, designations, or copyrights, and nothing contained in this Agreement will give LICENSEE any right, title, or interest in any of them.

(b)     Fees for Patents. In consideration for the exclusive license granted hereunder, LICENSEE agrees to promptly reimburse LICENSOR for that portion of LICENSOR' future legal fees and costs requested by LICENSOR which are incurred in filing for and obtaining any and all U.S. or international patents in the technologies incorporated into the TECHNOLOGY.

*(This requires the licensee to pay all patent maintenance fees.)*

(c)     Obligation to Protect. LICENSEE agrees to use reasonable efforts to protect LICENSOR' proprietary rights and to cooperate, at LICENSEE's expense, in LICENSOR' efforts to protect its proprietary rights. LICENSEE agrees to promptly notify LICENSOR of any known or suspected breach of LICENSOR' proprietary rights that comes to LICENSEE's attention.

*(This requires the licensee to use reasonable efforts to protect the TECHNOLOGY.)*

6.     No Assignment.

LICENSOR has entered into this Agreement with LICENSEE because of LICENSEE's commitments, and further because of LICENSOR' confidence in LICENSEE, which confidence is personal in nature. This Agreement will not be assignable by LICENSEE, and LICENSEE may not delegate its duties hereunder without the prior written consent of LICENSOR and any attempted assignment or delegation by LICENSEE will be void and of no effect. The provisions hereof shall be binding upon and inure to the benefit of the parties, their successors and permitted assigns.

*(This is a no assignment obligation because the parties have continuing obligations and they have entered into this relationship each depending on the other. In order for this provision to have full effect, the clause that any attempted assignment is void and no effect must be present.)*

7.    Duration and Termination of Agreement

(a)    Term. This Agreement is for a term of one year only. This Agreement will not be renewed or extended, and neither party expects this Agreement to be renewed beyond that date. Notwithstanding the provisions of this Section 7(a), this Agreement may be terminated prior to the expiration of its stated term as set forth below.

*(The term of one-year term is very unusual since there is not enough time to exploit the TECHNOLOGY. This agreement ends naturally at that point so neither party has any obligation or expectation for renewal beyond that.)*

(b)    LICENSOR Termination for Cause. LICENSOR may terminate this Agreement at any time prior to the expiration of its stated term in the event that:

(i)    LICENSEE defaults in any payment due to LICENSOR and such default continues unremedied for a period of ten (10) days following notice of such default; or

(ii)    LICENSEE is merged, consolidated, sells all or substantially all of its assets, or implements or suffers any substantial change in management or control.

*(This provides the licensor with rights to terminate short of the end of the natural term upon the occurrence of several events.)*

(c)    Automatic Termination. This Agreement terminates automatically, with no further act or action of either party, if a receiver is appointed for LICENSEE or its property, LICENSEE makes an assignment for the benefit of its creditors, any proceedings are commenced by, for or against LICENSEE under any bankruptcy, insolvency or debtor's relief law, or LICENSEE is liquidated or dissolved.

*(Automatic termination is not enforceable in a case of a filing under U.S. Bankruptcy Law.)*

(d)     Effect of Termination or Expiration. Upon termination or expiration of this Agreement:

*(The effect of termination or expiration is very important. Expiration occurs at the end of a natural term, in this case one year. Termination occurs upon a defined event short of the end of the natural term.)*

(i)     All outstanding compensation owed by LICENSEE for the TECHNOLOGY, including the pro-rationed portion of any calendar quarter, will automatically be accelerated so it becomes due and payable on the effective date of termination.

*(The five-year continuation period for right of inspection is somewhat long. This right is intended to make sure that all payments are made during the term of the agreements.)*

(ii)     For a period of five (5) years after the date of termination or expiration, LICENSEE shall make available to LICENSOR for inspection and copying all books and records of LICENSEE that pertain to LICENSEE's performance of and compliance with its obligations, warranties and representations under this Agreement.

(iii)     LICENSEE will cease using any LICENSOR trademark, trade name, logo, or destination.

*(This is important because it clearly requires LICENSEE to cease using any of the licensor's trademarks.)*

(e)     No Damages for Termination or Expiration. NEITHER LICENSOR NOR LICENSEE WILL BE LIABLE TO THE OTHER FOR DAMAGES OF ANY KIND, INCLUDING SPECIAL, INDIRECT, INCIDENTAL OR CONSEQUENTIAL DAMAGES, ON ACCOUNT OF THE TERMINATION OR EXPIRATION OF THIS AGREEMENT IN ACCORDANCE WITH THIS SECTION.

*(This is a disclaimer of consequential damages.)*

LICENSEE WAIVES ANY RIGHT IT MAY HAVE TO GET ANY COMPENSATION OR REPARATIONS ON TERMINATION OR EXPIRATION OF THIS AGREEMENT UNDER THE LAW OF ANY COUNTRY OR OTHERWISE, OTHER THAN AS EXPRESSLY PROVIDED IN THIS AGREEMENT. Neither LICENSOR nor LICENSEE will be liable to the other on account of termination or expiration of this Agreement for reimbursement or damages for the loss of goodwill, prospective profits or anticipated income, or on account of any expenditures, investments, leases or commitments made by either LICENSOR or LICENSEE or for any other reason whatsoever based upon or arising out of such termination or expiration. LICENSEE acknowledges that (i) LICENSEE has no expectation and has gotten no assurances that any investment by LICENSEE in the promotion of the TECHNOLOGY will be recovered or recouped or that LICENSEE will obtain any anticipated amount of profits by virtue of this agreement, and (ii) LICENSEE will not have or acquire by virtue of this Agreement or otherwise any vested, proprietary or other right in the promotion of the TECHNOLOGY or in "goodwill" created by its efforts hereunder. THE PARTIES ACKNOWLEDGE THAT THIS SECTION HAS BEEN INCLUDED AS A MATERIAL INDUCEMENT FOR LICENSOR TO ENTER INTO THIS AGREEMENT AND THAT LICENSOR WOULD NOT HAVE ENTERED INTO THIS AGREEMENT BUT FOR THE LIMITATIONS OF LIABILITY AS SET FORTH HEREIN.

*(This is intended to avoid any liability on the licensor if this agreement expires or is terminated prior to the licensee being able to fully exploit the TECHNOLOGY and generate a return on his investment. Again, it is unlikely that any licensee will accept a one-year term. This provision is primarily applicable to international transactions. Some foreign laws protect local agents and distributors against early termination or even expirations. This provision could be shortened significantly without creating any material risk for the licensor.)*

(f)    Survival.    LICENSOR' rights and LICENSEE's obligations to pay LICENSOR all amounts due hereunder, as well as LICENSEE's obligations under Sections 1(d), 2(e), (f), (g) and (j); 3, 5,

7(d), (e) and (f); 9, 10, 11, 12, and 13 will survive termination or expiration of this Agreement.

*(Survival is a very important provision since certain obligations such as payment and confidentiality need to extend beyond the termination or expiration of the agreement.)*

8.     Relationship of the Parties.

LICENSEE's relationship with LICENSOR during the term of this Agreement will be that of an independent contractor, LICENSEE will not have, and will not represent that it has, any power, right or authority to bind LICENSOR, or to assume or create any obligations or responsibility, express or implied, on behalf of LICENSOR or in LICENSOR' name, except as herein expressly provided.

9.     Indemnification.

(a)     Indemnification of LICENSOR. LICENSEE hereby indemnifies and agrees to hold LICENSOR harmless from any loss, liability, damages, costs or expense (including reasonable legal counsel fees), arising out of any claims or suits (including any product liability claims) which may be brought or made against LICENSOR for any alleged manufacturing defect or inherent dangers or design defects in products using or incorporating the TECHNOLOGY.

*(Subsection (a) is unusual because the licensee is identifying the licensor with respect to patent liability claims. Normally, there would be an indemnification by the licensor or warranty representation by the licensor as to intellectual property rights. The licensor would usually bear the primary obligation to protect the licensee with respect to the intellectual property rights in the TECHNOLOGY.)*

(b)     Products Liability Insurance Coverage. LICENSEE further agrees to obtain and maintain premiums for a product liability insurance policy covering damages or claims or attorney fees arising from any alleged design defects or inherent damages allegedly attributable to LICENSOR, in the amount of $_____, naming LICENSOR as an insured.

*(This is further back-up to protect the licensor with respect to product liability claims.)*

(c)     <u>No Combination Claims</u>. *LICENSOR is not liable for any patent infringement claims under this Agreement*. LICENSOR shall not be liable to LICENSEE for any claim arising from or based upon the combination, operation or use of the TECHNOLOGY with equipment or materials not supplied or recommended by LICENSOR, or arising from any alteration or modification of the TECHNOLOGY.

(d)     <u>Indemnification of LICENSOR for Other Causes</u>. In addition to indemnification as described in Section 9(a) above, LICENSEE further agrees to indemnify LICENSOR (including paying all reasonable attorneys' fees and costs of litigation) against and hold LICENSOR harmless from, any and all claims by any other party resulting from any of LICENSEE's acts, omissions, or misrepresentations, regardless of the form of action.

(e)     <u>Infringement by Third Parties</u>.

(i) LICENSEE agrees to use its best efforts to detect infringements of the TECHNOLOGY—and on discovery of any suspected infringement, LICENSEE will promptly notify LICENSOR of such infringement. LICENSEE may (at its own expense) take all necessary steps to protect the TECHNOLOGY but will not be obligated to do so. In the event LICENSEE initiates litigation relating to the TECHNOLOGY, LICENSOR agrees to assist and cooperate with LICENSEE in such litigation, at licensee's expense. LICENSOR will not be obligated, however, in any way to provide LICENSEE with financial assistance for protecting and defending such patent or patents. In the event that LICENSEE prosecutes infringers, the recovery of damages will be shared equally by LICENSEE and LICENSOR.

(ii) If LICENSEE elects not to prosecute infringers, LICENSOR will have the right to do so at its own expense, but all recovery of damages will then be retained by LICENSOR.

(f)     Infringement of Third Party Patents. LICENSOR believes that none of the TECHNOLOGY infringes upon rights that any third person may have acquired with regard to any other invention. In the event that LICENSEE is sued for infringement of any patent or other intellectual property right, by reason of its making, using or selling products using or incorporating the TECHNOLOGY, then LICENSOR will not be liable for any costs of defending such action or for any damages awarded. LICENSOR' sole liability under any action regarding the TECHNOLOGY will be limited solely to cooperation with LICENSEE in defending such action.

*(This deals with LICENSOR' obligations with respect to infringement of third-party patents, LICENSOR attempts to limit his liability to cooperation and to have no other liability. It is highly improbable that the licensor would be able to avoid liability that easily. The licensee would usually want the licensor to stand fully behind the intellectual property rights in the TECHNOLOGY.)*

10.   Disclaimer of Warranties.

*(This is a disclaimer of warranties both as to the performance of the TECHNOLOGY and as to non-infringement. This is a very broad disclaimer of warranties, one that a licensee is likely to negotiate to gain a higher level of assurance.)*

(a)     Disclaimer of Warranties. LICENSOR MAKES NO WARRANTIES OR REPRESENTATIONS AS TO PERFORMANCE OF THE TECHNOLOGY TO LICENSEE OR TO ANY OTHER PERSON. TO THE EXTENT PERMITTED BY APPLICABLE LAW, ALL IMPLIED WARRANTIES, INCLUDING BUT NOT LIMITED TO IMPLIED WARRANTIES OF MERCHANTABILITY, FITNESS FOR A PARTICULAR PURPOSES AND NONINFRINGEMENT, ARE HEREBY EXCLUDED BY LICENSOR.

(b)     LICENSEE Warranty. LICENSEE agrees not to make any warranty, guarantee or representation, whether written or oral, on LICENSOR' behalf.

11.   Limited Liability.

*(This is another limitation of liability provision that is a duplication of Section 7(e). It also purports to disclaim "direct" damages which is not likely enforceable. The language at the beginning which is intended to address the issue of what happens if a warranty fails of its essential purposes is not applicable since Section 10(a) does not make any warranties.)*

(a)  REGARDLESS WHETHER ANY REMEDY SET FORTH HEREIN FAILS OF ITS ESSENTIAL PURPOSE OR OTHERWISE, LICENSOR WILL NOT BE LIABLE FOR ANY LOST PROFITS OR FOR ANY INDIRECT, SPECIAL, INCIDENTAL, CONSEQUENTIAL, PUNITIVE OR OTHER SPECIAL DAMAGES SUFFERED BY LICENSEE, ITS CUSTOMERS OR OTHERS ARISING OUT OF OR RELATED TO THIS AGREEMENT.

12.  Protection of Proprietary Rights.

LICENSOR and LICENSEE acknowledge that the TECHNOLOGY is of a character which is or may be protectable by patent, trade secrecy, and/or copyright under the laws of the United States and other countries. LICENSOR agrees to cooperate with LICENSEE in obtaining patent, trademark, copyright, and other statutory protections for the TECHNOLOGY at LICENSEE's expense, and LICENSOR hereby authorizes LICENSEE to execute in LICENSEE's name an application for patent or copyright registration of the TECHNOLOGY and such other documents of registration and recordation as may be necessary to perfect in LICENSEE the rights granted LICENSEE hereunder in each country in which the TECHNOLOGY is sold, distributed, or sublicensed. All proprietary rights in any portion of any derivative work or improvement based on the TECHNOLOGY will be owned exclusively by LICENSEE. LICENSOR hereby authorizes LICENSEE to use the trademarks and trade names of LICENSEE's choosing in marketing the TECHNOLOGY.

13.  Nondisclosure.

LICENSEE and LICENSOR agree that the terms and conditions of this Agreement, the concepts, know-how and techniques known or developed by LICENSOR at the time of entering into this agreement, any other information concerning either party's marketing plans, existing or future products (including the TECHNOLOGY), and any other confidential business or technical information disclosed in the furtherance of this Agreement will be deemed confidential to the disclosing party and held in strict confidence and will not be disseminated or disclosed without the express written consent of the disclosing party. Notwithstanding the above, the following materials will not be deemed confidential:

*(Nondisclosure needs to be reviewed from the licensee's point of view to determine if the actual sale of products requires a nondisclosure obligation. The licensee must be able to exploit the TECHNOLOGY the way it is commercially anticipated, such as for mass marketed products when no signed agreement is possible.*

*Exclusions from the definition of what is confidential are not standard. Here, there are three different exclusions which are not unusual but there can be others. Once common exclusion would be when the invention or TECHNOLOGY was developed independently by the licensee.)*

(a) Information which at the time of disclosure is in the public domain;

(b) Information which after disclosure is published or otherwise becomes part of the public domain through no fault of either party (but only after, and only to the extent that, it is published or otherwise becomes a part of the public domain);

(c) Information which can be shown was gotten from a third party who did not acquire it, directly or indirectly, under an obligation of confidence.

14.    Trademarks.

Any trademarks used by LICENSOR to identify the TECHNOLOGY, except for LICENSOR' name, are hereby assigned by LICENSOR to LICENSEE. Any trademarks adopted and used by LICENSEE in the marketing of the TECHNOLOGY will be the sole property of LICENSEE. LICENSEE will have the sole responsibility for ensuring that any such trademarks do not infringe the rights of third parties.

15.     Consequential Damages.

Under no other circumstances will either party to this agreement will be liable to the other party for incidental or consequential damages or the loss of anticipated profits arising from any breach of this Agreement by the other party even if notice is given of the possibility of such damages.

16.     General Terms.

(a)     Entire Agreement. This Agreement and the Exhibits attached hereto state the entire agreement between the parties with respect to this license. No amendment or modification of this agreement may be made except by an instrument in writing signed by both parties.

(b)     Assignment. This Agreement may not be assigned in whole or in party by LICENSEE without the prior written consent of LICENSOR, which consent will not be unreasonably withheld. LICENSOR may assign LICENSOR' interest in all or part of the payments due LICENSOR hereunder upon notice in writing to LICENSEE.

*(Assignment as a partial duplication of Section 6. This does add the right for the licensor to assign its payments rights but not the whole agreement.)*

(c)     Governing Law. This Agreement will be governed and interpreted in accordance with the laws of the State of California, excluding that body of law known as conflicts of law. Except as herein otherwise provided, the parties agree that any dispute arising under this Agreement will be resolved in the state or federal courts within the State of California and LICENSEE expressly consents to jurisdiction therein. Venue for any legal action will be the state courts of

Sacramento County, California, and the federal courts of the Northern District of California.

(d)     Notice. Any notice required or permitted to be sent hereunder will be deemed delivered on the date mailed or otherwise dispatched if mailed, postage prepaid, by registered, express or certified mail, return receipt requested, or by nationally-recognized private express courier, to either party at the address listed above, or such other addresses of which either party may so notify the other.

(e)     Independent Contractor. LICENSOR will be deemed to have the status of an independent contractor to LICENSEE, and nothing in this Agreement will be deemed to place the parties in the relationship of employer-employee, principal-agent, partners or joint venturers.

(f)     Attorney's Fees. In the event that any legal action, including arbitration, is required in order to enforce or interpret any of the provisions of this Agreement, the prevailing party in such action will recover all reasonable costs and expenses, including attorney's fees, incurred in connection therewith.

(g)     Waiver. The failure of either party to enforce any provision of this Agreement will not be deemed a waiver of that or any other provision of this Agreement.

(h)     Force Majeure. Neither party will be deemed in default of this Agreement to the extent that performance of their obligations or attempts to cure any breach are delayed or prevented by reason of any act of God, fire, natural disaster, accident, act of government, shortages of material or supplies, or any other cause beyond the control of such party, provided that such party gives the other party written notice thereof promptly and, in any event, within 15 days of discovery thereof and uses its good faith efforts to cure the breach. In the event of such a Force Majeure, the time for performance or cure will be extended for a period equal to the duration of the Force Majeure but not in excess of 6 months.

(i)    <u>Headings</u>. The headings of the Sections of this Agreement are for convenience only and will not be of any effect in construing the meanings of the Paragraphs.

IN WITNESS WHEREOF, the parties hereto have executed this agreement as of the date first written above.

XYZ Corporation

By: _____(LICENSEE'S SIGNATURE)_____

Its: _____(SIGNOR'S TITLE)_____

By: _____(LICENSOR'S SIGNATURE)_____

# Sample Nondisclosure Agreement

This Agreement is effective this _____ day of ____*(effective date)*_____,
20__, by and between _____*(your name)*_____ , hereinafter called
LICENSOR, having his/her principal address at _____*(your*
*address)*_____, and XYZ Corporation, a _____*(name of state)*_____
corporation, hereinafter called LICENSEE, having its principal
address at _____*(LICENSEE'S ADDRESS)*_____.

*LICENSOR is in the business of applied research and technology development and acquisition in the field of*
*_____. In order to pursue mutual business opportunities, LICENSEE and LICENSOR agree there*
*is a need for LICENSOR to disclose such Confidential Information which LICENSEE agrees not to disclose or utilize*
*in any way except for the Business Purpose, defined as the economic and technical evaluation of technology licensing or*
*purchasing such technology.*

In consideration of the disclosure of such Information by
LICENSOR, LICENSEE agrees as follows:

*(This NDA is a preliminary NDA for the purpose of a potential assignee or licensee to evaluate the TECHNOLOGY*
*for either purchasing or licensing it.*

*There is no standard NDA. All NDA's are different and have to be read carefully.*

*The first issue is to look at the definition of the recipient to make sure that it does not include more than one party such as a*
*group of corporations as opposed to a single corporation.*

*This nondisclosure agreement only runs one way, that is, from LICENSOR to LICENSEE. It does not cover any*
*information provided by the licensee to the licensor. A nondisclosure agreement for use one way should not be just simply*
*adapted to be used for a mutual arrangement. It should be carefully thought through and drafted.)*

1. This Agreement will apply to all Confidential Information disclosed
by LICENSOR to LICENSEE including but not limited to the
following:

*(This contains the definition of confidential and proprietary information. From LICENSOR point of view, the definition*
*should be established very broadly by generally describing the TECHNOLOGY and then having confidential information*
*being anything relating to such TECHNOLOGY.)*

2. LICENSEE agrees to hold LICENSOR's Confidential Information
in strict confidence, not to disclose it to any third party, and not to use
any Confidential Information for any purpose except the Business
Purpose.

*(This provision covers the obligation not to disclose or use any confidential information. Sometimes nondisclosure agreements fail to cover use restrictions.)*

3. Confidential Information will not include information which is (i) now or hereafter, becomes through no act or failure to act on the part of LICENSEE, generally known to the public; (ii) was acquired by LICENSEE before receiving such information from LICENSOR and without restriction as to use or disclosure; (iii) is hereafter rightfully furnished to LICENSEE by a third party without restriction to use or disclosure; or (iv) is disclosed with the prior written consent of LICENSOR.

*(This provision contains the exclusions from the definition of confidential information. Anything covered by the exclusion would not have to be held confidential by the recipient.)*

4. Upon LICENSOR's request, LICENSEE will return all Confidential Information to LICENSOR.

5. LICENSEE agrees that nothing contained in this Agreement will be construed as granting any right to LICENSEE, by license or otherwise, to any Confidential Information.

6. LICENSEE agrees that all Confidential Information is owned solely by LICENSOR (or its licensors) and that the unauthorized disclosure or use of such Confidential Information would cause irreparable harm and significant injury, the degree of which may be difficult to ascertain. Accordingly, LICENSEE agrees that LICENSOR has the right to obtain an immediate injunction enjoining any breach of this Agreement, as well as the right to pursue any and all other rights and remedies available at law or in equity for such a breach.

*(This provision strengthens the licensor's position in the event that it desires to obtain injunctive or similar type equitable relief if there is a breach of this nondisclosure agreement.)*

7. This Agreement will be construed, interpreted, and applied in accordance with the laws of California (excluding its body of law controlling conflicts of laws). This Agreement is the complete and exclusive statement regarding the subject matter of this Agreement and

supersedes all prior Agreements, understandings and communications, oral or written.

*(The entire agreement provision is to make sure that the written agreement controls and may not be amended by verbal statements.)*

8. This Agreement shall remain in effect for seven years from the date of the last disclosure of Confidential Information, at which time it will terminate.

IN WITNESS WHEREOF, the parties hereto have executed this Agreement by their duly authorized officers or representatives.

LICENSEE, _____

_____ (printed name)

_____ (title)

_____ (date)

LICENSOR, _____

*(This covers the duration of the agreement which is very important to the disclosure of the information. The recipient will usually try to restrict the length of its obligations to as short a period as possible. The discloser of information, LICENSOR, wants to protect the information as long as possible.*

*This agreement does not require anything provided in tangible form to be marked as confidential, although that is a common requirement. It also does not require any information that is disclosed verbally to be summarized in writing and delivered to the other party. In some cases, the recipient will not have any obligation of nondisclosure unless the information is marked confidential. In the case of a verbal disclosure, in some cases, the recipient will not have any obligation unless the information is indicated to be confidential at the time of the verbal disclosure and there is a follow-up written notification of confidentiality written in a certain period after the verbal disclosure.)*

# Company Nondisclosure Agreement

*(For use when you, (RECEIVER) agree not to disclose certain information received from another party (DISCLOSER)*

This Agreement is effective this _____ day of _____*(effective date)*_____, 20___, by and between _____*(your name)*_____ , hereinafter called DISCLOSER, having his/her principal address at _____*(your address)*_____, and XYZ Corporation, a _____*(name of state)*_____ corporation, hereinafter called RECEIVER, having its principal address at _____*(RECEIVER'S ADDRESS)*_____.

RECEIVER is in the business of _____ and Company is in the business specified in Exhibit A. In order to pursue the mutual business purpose specified in Exhibit A (the "Business Purpose"), Company and RECEIVER recognize that there is a need to disclose to one another certain confidential information of each party to be used only for the Business Purpose and to protect such confidential information from unauthorized use and disclosure.

In consideration of other party's disclosure of such information, each party agrees as follows:

1. This Agreement will apply to all confidential and proprietary information disclosed by one party to the other party, including information listed in Exhibit A and other information which the disclosing party identifies in writing as confidential before or within thirty days after disclosure to the receiving party ("Confidential Information").

2. Each party agrees (i) to hold the other party's Confidential Information in strict confidence, (ii) not to disclose such Confidential Information to any other third parties, and (iii) not to use any Confidential Information for any purpose except for the Business Purpose. Each party may disclose the other party's Confidential Information to its responsible employees with a bona fide need to

know, but only to the extent necessary to carry out the Business Purpose. Each party agrees to instruct all such employees not to disclose such Confidential Information to third parties, including consultants, without the prior written permission of the disclosing party.

3.      Confidential Information will not include information which:

(i)      is now or, hereafter becomes, through no act or failure to act on the part of the receiving party, generally known or available to the public;

(ii)      was known by RECEIVER prior to receiving such information from DISCLOSER;

(iii)      was acquired by RECEIVER before receiving such information from DISCLOSER and without restrictions as to use or disclosure;

(iv)      is hereafter rightfully furnished to RECEIVER by a third party;

(v)      has been independently developed by RECEIVER;

(vi)      is required to be disclosed pursuant to any law or regulation; or

(vii)      is disclosed with the prior written consent of RECEIVER.

4.      Upon DISCLOSER's request, RECEIVER will promptly return to DISCLOSER all tangible items containing or consisting of DISCLOSER's Confidential Information and all copies thereof.

5.     RECEIVER recognizes and agrees that nothing contained in this Agreement will be construed as granting any rights to RECEIVER, by license or otherwise, to any Confidential Information except as specified in this Agreement.

6.     This Agreement will be construed, interpreted, and applied in accordance with the laws of the State of California (excluding its body of law controlling conflicts of law). This Agreement and Exhibit A attached hereto are the complete and exclusive statement regarding the subject matter of this Agreement and supersede all prior agreements, understandings, and communications, oral or written, between the parties regarding the subject matter of this Agreement.

7.     This Agreement will remain in effect for three years from the date first set forth above, at which time it will terminate.

**IN WITNESS WHEREOF**, the parties hereto have executed this Agreement by their duly authorized officers or representatives.

**RECEIVER:**

**Signature:** _____

**Typed Name:** _____

**Title:** _____

**DISCLOSER:**

**Signature:** _____

**Typed Name:** _____

**Title:** _____

**EXHIBIT A**

1.     Business of DISCLOSER:
2.     Business Purpose:
3.     Confidential Information of DISCLOSER:

# Mutual Nondisclosure Agreement

*(For use when two parties agree not to disclose information provided by the other other)*

This Agreement is effective this _____ day of _____*(effective date)*_____, 20___, by and between _____*(your name)*_____ , hereinafter called PARTY-A, having his/her principal address at _____*(your address)*_____, and _____*(your name)*_____ , hereinafter called PARTY-B, having his/her principal address at _____*(your address)* _____.

PARTY-A is in the business of _____, and PARTY-B is in the business specified in Exhibit A. In order to pursue the mutual business purpose specified in Exhibit A (the "Business Purpose"), PARTY-B and PARTY-A recognize that there is a need to disclose to one another certain confidential information of each party to be used only for the Business Purpose and to protect such confidential information from unauthorized use and disclosure.

In consideration of other party's disclosure of such information, each party agrees as follows:

1. This Agreement will apply to all confidential and proprietary information disclosed by one party to the other party, including information listed in Exhibit A and other information which the disclosing party identifies in writing as confidential before or within thirty days after disclosure to the receiving party ("Confidential Information").

2. Each party agrees (i) to hold the other party's Confidential Information in strict confidence, (ii) not to disclose such Confidential Information to any other third parties, and (iii) not to use any Confidential Information for any purpose except for the Business Purpose. Each party may disclose the other party's Confidential Information to its responsible employees with a bona fide need to

know, but only to the extent necessary to carry out the Business Purpose. Each party agrees to instruct all such employees not to disclose such Confidential Information to third parties, including consultants, without the prior written permission of the disclosing party.

3.      Confidential Information will not include information which:

(i)      is now or, hereafter becomes, through no act or failure to act on the part of the receiving party, generally known or available to the public;

(ii)      was acquired by the receiving party before receiving such information from the disclosing party and without restriction as to use or disclosure;

(iii)      is hereafter rightfully furnished to the receiving party by a third party, without restriction as to use or disclosure;

(iv)      is information which the receiving party can document was independently developed by the receiving party;

(v)      is required to be disclosed pursuant to the law, provided the receiving party uses reasonable efforts to give the disclosing party reasonable notice if such required disclosure; or

(vi)      is disclosed with the prior written consent of the disclosing party.

4.      Each party agrees not to remove any of the other party's Confidential Information from the premises of the disclosing party without the disclosing party's prior written approval. Each party agrees to exercise extreme care in protecting the confidentiality of any Confidential Information which is removed, only with the disclosing party's prior written approval, from the disclosing party's premises. Each party agrees to comply with any and all terms and conditions the

disclosing party may impose upon any such approved removal, such as conditions that the removed Confidential Information and all copies must be returned by a certain date, and that no copies are to be made off of the premises.

5.     Upon the disclosing party's request, the receiving party will promptly return to the disclosing party all tangible items containing or consisting of the disclosing party's Confidential Information and all copies thereof.

6.     Each party recognizes and agree that nothing contained in this Agreement will be construed as granting any rights to the receiving party, by license or otherwise, to any of the disclosing party's Confidential Information except as specified in this Agreement.

7.     Each party acknowledges that all of the disclosing party's Confidential Information is owned solely by the disclosing party (or its licensors) and that the unauthorized disclosure or user of such Confidential Information would cause irreparable harm and significant injury, the degree of which may be difficult to ascertain. Accordingly, each party agrees that the disclosing party will have the right to obtain an immediate injunction enjoining any breach of this Agreement, as well as the right to pursue any and all other rights and remedies available at law or in equity for such a breach.

8.     This Agreement will be construed, interpreted, and applied in accordance with the laws of the State of California (excluding its body of law controlling conflicts of laws). Subject to terms and conditions regarding the removal of Confidential Information as set forth under Section 4, this Agreement and Exhibit A attached hereto are the complete and exclusive statement regarding the subject matter of this Agreement and supersede all prior agreements, understandings, and communications, oral or written, between the parties regarding the subject matter of this Agreement.

9. This Agreement will remain in effect for five years from the date of the last disclosure of Confidential Information at which time it will terminate.

**IN WITNESS WHEREOF**, the parties hereto have executed this Agreement by their duly authorized officers or representatives.

**PARTY-A:**

**Signature:** _____

**Typed Name:** _____

**Title:** _____

**PARTY-B:**

**Signature:** _____

**Typed Name:** _____

**Title:** _____

## EXHIBIT A

1. Business of PARTY-B:

2. Business Purpose:

3. Confidential Information of PARTY-A:

4. Confidential Information of PARTY-B:

# Nondisclosure Agreement

*(For use when you, (DISCLOSER) wish to reveal certain information to another party (RECEIVER) and they agree not to divulge that information.)*

This Agreement is effective this \_\_\_\_\_ day of \_\_\_\_*(effective date)*_____, 20\_\_, by and between _____*(your name)*_____ , hereinafter called RECEIVER, having his/her principal address at _____*(your address)*_____, and XYZ Corporation, a \_\_\_\_\_*(name of state)*\_\_\_\_\_ corporation, hereinafter called DISCLOSER, having its principal address at _____*(DISCLOSER'S ADDRESS)*_____.

DISCLOSER is in the business of _____ and RECEIVER is in the business specified in Exhibit A. In order to pursue the mutual business purpose specified in Exhibit A (the "Business Purpose"), RECEIVER and DISCLOSER recognize that there is a need to disclose to one another certain confidential information of each party to be used only for the Business Purpose and to protect such confidential information from unauthorized use and disclosure.

In consideration of the disclosure of such information by DISCLOSER, RECEIVER agrees as follows:

1. This Agreement will apply to all confidential and proprietary information disclosed by DISCLOSER to RECEIVER, including but not limited to the information listed in Exhibit A ("Confidential Information").

2. RECEIVER agrees (i) to hold DISCLOSER'S Confidential Information in strict confidence, (ii) not to disclose such Confidential Information to any other third parties, and (iii) not to use any Confidential Information for any purpose except for the Business Purpose. Each party may disclose the other party's Confidential Information to its responsible employees with a bona fide need to

know, but only to the extent necessary to carry out the Business Purpose. RECEIVER agrees to instruct all such employees not to disclose such Confidential Information to third parties, including consultants, without the prior written permission of DISCLOSER.

3.      Confidential Information will not include information which:

(i)      is now or, hereafter becomes, through no act or failure to act on the part of RECEIVER, generally known or available to the public;

(ii)      was acquired by RECEIVER before receiving such information from DISCLOSER and without restriction as to use or disclosure;

(iii)      is hereafter rightfully furnished to RECEIVER by a third party, without restriction as to use or disclosure; or

(iv)      is disclosed with the prior written consent of DISCLOSER.

4.      RECEIVER agrees not to remove any Confidential Information from the premises of DISCLOSER without DISCLOSER's prior written approval. RECEIVER agrees to exercise extreme care in protecting the confidentiality of any Confidential Information which is removed, only with DISCLOSER's prior written approval, from DISCLOSER's premises. RECEIVER agrees to comply with any and all terms and conditions DISCLOSER may impose upon any such approved removal, such as conditions that the removed Confidential Information and all copies must be returned by a certain date, and that no copies are to be made off of DISCLOSER's premises.

5.      Upon DISCLOSER's request, RECEIVER will promptly return to DISCLOSER all tangible items containing or

consisting of DISCLOSER's Confidential Information and all copies thereof.

6.     RECEIVER recognizes and agrees that nothing contained in this Agreement will be construed as granting any rights to RECEIVER, by license or otherwise, to any Confidential Information except as specified in this Agreement.

7.     RECEIVER acknowledges that all Confidential Information is owned solely by DISCLOSER (or its licensors) and that the unauthorized disclosure or user of such Confidential Information would cause irreparable harm and significant injury, the degree if which may be difficult to ascertain. Accordingly, RECEIVER agrees that DISCLOSER will have the right to obtain an immediate injunction enjoining any breach of this Agreement, as well as the right to pursue any and all other rights and remedies available at law or in equity for such a breach.

8.     This Agreement will be construed, interpreted, and applied in accordance with the laws of the State of California (excluding its body of law controlling conflicts of laws). Subject to terms and conditions regarding the removal of Confidential Information from DISCLOSER's premises as set forth under Section 4, this Agreement and Exhibit A attached hereto are the complete and exclusive statement regarding the subject matter of this Agreement and supersede all prior agreements, understandings, and communications, oral or written, between the parties regarding the subject matter of this Agreement.

9.     This Agreement will remain in effect for five years from the date of the last disclosure of Confidential Information at which time it will terminate.

**IN WITNESS WHEREOF**, the parties hereto have executed this Agreement by their duly authorized officers or representatives.

**RECEIVER**

Signature: _____

Typed Name: _____

Title: _____

**DISCLOSER**

Signature: _____

Typed Name: _____

Title: _____

## EXHIBIT A

1.  Business of RECEIVER:

2.  Business Purpose:

3.  Confidential Information:

www.ingramcontent.com/pod-product-compliance
Lightning Source LLC
Chambersburg PA
CBHW070350220526
45467CB00001B/313